Anonymous

Message of His Excellency,

Richard Yates, Governor of Illinois, to the General Assembly, Jan. 2, 1865

Anonymous

Message of His Excellency,
Richard Yates, Governor of Illinois, to the General Assembly, Jan. 2, 1865

ISBN/EAN: 9783337810344

Printed in Europe, USA, Canada, Australia, Japan

Cover: Foto ©ninafisch / pixelio.de

More available books at **www.hansebooks.com**

MESSAGE

OF HIS EXCELLENCY,

RICHARD YATES,

GOVERNOR OF ILLINOIS,

TO THE

GENERAL ASSEMBLY.

JANUARY 2, 1865

SPRINGFIELD:
BAKER & PHILLIPS, PRINTERS.

1865.

MESSAGE.

Gentlemen of the General Assembly :

INTRODUCTION.

In delivering to you the last message which it devolves upon me, as the executive of the State, to communicate to the General Assembly, I feel it to be our first duty to render thanks to Almighty God for the continued protection and goodness of his Providence, for the abounding blessings with which He has favored us as a State, and for the continuance to us, unimpaired, the possession and enjoyment of our civil and religious liberty. For though a sad and waasting war has prevailed in the land, and thousands of homes and hearthstones have been made desolate, our government has been preserved to us, our nationality has been maintained unbroken, and our free institutions have come out of the shock of battle, not only not destroyed, or impaired, but stronger, and dearer to us than ever before. The storms of revolution, which have so rudely beat around the tree of liberty, have served only to deepen its roots and strengthen its trunk, and the people at home stand reassured with new and unfaltering confidence in our institutions, while foreign nationalities are forced to pay the tribute of involuntary respect to a people who, true to the memories and traditions of their fathers, and faithful to the sacred trust of liberty committed to their care, stand unappalled by the dark events of the gigantic war in which they have been engaged.

As a State, notwithstanding the war, we have prospered beyond all former precedents. Notwithstanding nearly two hundred thousand of the most athletic and vigorous of our population have been withdrawn from the field of production, the area of land now under cultivation is greater than at any former period, and the census of 1865 will exhibit an astonishing increase in every department of material industry and advancement; in a great increase of agricultural, manufacturing and mechanical wealth; in new and improved modes for production of every kind; in the substitution of machinery for the manual labor withdrawn by the war; in the triumphs of invention; in the wonderful increase of railroad enterprise; in the universal activity of business, in all its branches; in the rapid growth of our cities and villages; in the bountiful harvests, and in an unexampled material prosperity, prevailing on every hand; while, at the same time, the educational institutions of the people have in no way declined. Our colleges and schools, of every class and grade, are in the most flourishing condition; our benevolent institutions, State and private, are kept up and maintained; and, in a word, our prosperity is as complete and ample as though no tread of armies or beat of drum had been heard in all our borders.

I submit herewith a statement of the permanent debt, funded and unfunded, of the State.

There has been purchased and paid off by the State, with the Central Railroad Fund, from December 1, 1862, to December 15, 1864, State indebtedness, as follows:

Principal..	$875,988 41
Interest, arrears of interest, etc.................	30,158 98
	$906,147 39
10 per cent. paid on registered canal bonds, by Canal Trustees, installments July, 1863 and July 1864, 5 per cent. each......................	289,133 33
	$1,195,280 72

PERMANENT DEBT, FUNDED AND UNFUNDED.

Statement, showing amount of different classes of State indebtedness outstanding, Dec. 16, 1864:

Illinois Bank and Internal Improvement stock,....	$31,000 00
Illinois Internal Improvement stock,............	42,000 00
Internal Improvement scrip,....................	19,570 33
Liquidation bonds,............................	234,650 21

New Internal Improvement stock.............. 1,848,407 85
Interest bonds, 1847,..................... 1,206,836 96
Interest stock, 1857,..................... 701,404 75
Two certificates for arrears of interest,.......... 1002 58
Refunded stock,........................ 1,837,000 00
Normal University bonds,................... 65,000 00
Thornton Loan bonds, (act app. Feb. 21, 1861),... 182,000 00
Balance Canal claims, under Thornton Loan act,.. 3624 58
War bonds,........................... 1,679,100 00
Illinois and Michigan Canal bonds, payable in New
York,............................. 1,618,000 00
Illinois and Michigan Canal bonds, payable in
London,............................ 1,631,688 89
Interest certificates, Canal stock, not registered,.. 17,661 33
Canal scrip, signed by Governor,.............. 2616 97
121 Macallister and Stebbins bonds, which, accord-
ing to statement of C. Macallister, would amount,
Jan. 1, 1865, to about.................. 57,000 00

$11,178,564 45

STATE DEBT.

Since December 1, 1862, in addition to the regular semi-annual
payments of accruing interest on the State debt, the following
amounts have been liquidated, with the proceeds of the fund derived from the Illinois Central Railroad, viz:

Refunded stock of 1860, redeemed under the Governor's proclamation of September 28,'1863, including
accrued interest on the same,................. $68,507 50
State bonds, purchased at par, canceled and deposited
with the Auditor, the principal and interest of
which amount to... .... 706,182 12
Scrip, coupons, etc., paid off at par, under the act of
February 22, 1861,...................... 23,643 36

Amount of principal and interest extinguished with
the Central Railroad fund, from December 1, 1862,
to November 30, 1864,..................... $798,332 98

In addition to this, a further amount of $107,815 42, of the
same fund, has been used in the purchase of State indebtedness,
since December 1st, making, in the whole, $906,148 40 of the
public debt extinguished in a little over two years. The amount
derived from the two-mill tax, on the assessment of the year 1863,

applicable to dividend on State indebtedness, presented to the Auditor January 1st, 1865, is some six hundred thousand dollars. This, added to the amount extinguished with the Central Railroad fund, makes an aggregate of one and a half millions of payment on the debt of the State, since December 1, 1862. And the indications of increased receipts from the Central Railroad, and from the two-mill tax, are such as to warrant the belief that at least one million of dollars, per annum, will be hereafter realized from these two sources.

RECEIPTS FROM THE CENTRAL RAILROAD.

The amount received from the Central Railroad, for the seven per cent. on the gross earnings of said company, of the past two years, has been as follows :

For the six months ending April 30, 1863..........$126,634 83
For the six months ending October 31, 1863......... 173,759 75
For the six months ending April 30, 1864........... 170,055 08
For the six months ending October 31, 1864......... 235,458 96

$705,908 62

It will be seen that the amount received for per centage on the earnings of 1864 is more than one-third larger than that for 1863.

REVENUE—RECEIPTS AND EXPENDITURES.

The receipts into the treasury for revenue purposes, for two years, ending November 30, 1864, have been $497,616 11 ; of which amount $109,547 64 was received for tax levied in the year 1862, and $315,088 46 for tax levied in the year 1863 ; the remainder of the amount received being from miscellaneous sources. The amount in the treasury, December 1, 1862, was $374,697 19, which, added to the amount received, makes an aggregate of $872,303 30.

The amount of warrants drawn against this fund, from December 1, 1862, to November 30, 1864, is $884,014 97, and the amount of the same outstanding, unpaid December 1, 1864, as appears from the Auditor's report, was $20,510 98. It will be seen that a continuation of the expenditures, in the same ratio, as for the past two years, and of the receipts from taxation, as for the collection for 1863, will result in a deficiency of the receipts, as compared with the expenditures, of more than one hundred thousand dollars per annum; and this, without considering the greatly enhanced prices necessary to be paid for all articles purchased for the use of the State, and of all services rendered, except such as the compensation for which is fixed in amount.

The rate of tax now levied for revenue purposes is one and one-fifth mill on the dollar of valuation, producing, for the year 1863, (as before stated) $315,088 46 of actual receipts at the treasury, whilst one-half of the amount expended in two years will be found to be $442,007 48. The conclusion is obvious that an increase of taxation or a reduction of expenditures is of absolute necessity.

COLLECTION OF TAXES.

The act of the last General Assembly authorizing the collection of taxes in legal tender notes and postal currency expired, by limitation, on the 1st of January, 1865, thus leaving the act of 1853 in force; which act requires payment of taxes in gold and silver. I presume that no argument is needed to show that a re-enactment of the law authorizing payment of taxes in United States notes is a matter not only of public policy but of absolute necessity.

APPROPRIATION ACT OF FEBRUARY 14, 1863.

The act of the last General Assembly, approved February 14, 1863, entitled "An act to provide for the ordinary and contingent expenses of the government until the adjournment of the next regular session of the General Assembly," and containing provisions for the payment of the incidental and contingent expenses of the government and of the different State departments, clerk hire of the different State officers, etc., and in aid of sick and wounded Illinois soldiers, has been pronounced by the Supreme Court to be void. Previous to the rendering of this decision several warrants had been issued by the Auditor, for purposes contemplated by said act; none of which have been paid. In fact, the decision of the Supreme Court was rendered in suits brought against the Treasurer, with the view of compelling him to make payment of said warrants. All these warrants were regularly issued by the Auditor, on accounts for services actually rendered and articles actually furnished; and all of the same should rightfully be paid. The aggregate amount of such warrants is less than seven thousand dollars. The cost of clerk hire and incidental expenses of the several State departments have been borne by the State officers, from private means, for the past two years ; and I would therefore recommend the re-enactment of the law, with a provision legalizing the warrants outstanding, and requiring the State Treasurer to treat the same, in all respects, in like manner with warrants issued under other laws.

It will be recollected, in this connection, that in June, 1863, a disagreement having occurred between the two Houses of the the General Assembly as to the time of adjournment, I availed myself of the power vested in me by the constitution, to prorogue them. Seeing, as I supposed, a disposition to embarrass the government in the prosecution of the war, and a refusal to make the necessary appropriations to carry on the State government, and provide aid for the relief of our sick and wounded soldiers, and also to interfere with the prerogatives of the State Executive, I deemed it my duty to avail myself of the contingency which the constitution placed in my hands, of rescuing our noble State from obloquy, by a prorogation of the General Assembly. It will be seen, however, that such a necessity, and the subsequent decision of the Supreme Court, declaring the said law, making the contingent appropriations aforesaid void, devolved upon the State authorities the alternative of raising the means necessary to carry on the government, by advances from private citizens, which would necessarily be large, by reason of greatly increased service and expenditures in every department of the government, growing out of the complications of the war. I therefore recommend the re-enactment of the said law, with a clause for adjusting and paying all accounts for expenditures incurred, as above stated, to be audited by the Auditor, and warrants issued, upon the approval of the Governor.

I herewith submit a report of the expenses incurred in my office, and other necessary expenses, incurred according to the intent of said appropriation.

Much credit is due to liberal and patriotic citizens of Chicago, Springfield and Knox county, for advances made by them so generously to the State, in its emergency.

ARMY AUDITING BOARD.

I submit herewith the final report of the Board of Army Auditors, appointed under the "Act creating a war fund and to provide for auditing all accounts and disbursements arising under the call for volunteers." It embodies a detailed statement showing the dates of all claims filed, names of the parties filing the same, their amounts, what for, and amounts allowed; also the amount of claims rejected, suspended, withdrawn, barred, etc. The report is valuable, and should be published.

BARRED WAR ACCOUNTS.

Under the fifth section of the act of May 2, 1861, creating a war fund, and providing for auditing accounts of war expenses, all claims for such expenses were required to be presented for adjustment within three months from the accruing of the same—in default of which, such accounts were required to be "considered donated to the State, and not thereafter allowed, under any pretense whatever." This provision of the law has, in many instances, worked very great hardship. Many persons furnished articles, and rendered service, in utter ignorance of this provision of the law, and others were ordered away from the State, in the military service, and had not the opportunity to present their claims until long after the three months had expired.

The Board of Commissioners, wishing to do all that lay in their power to facilitate the collection of claims which they considered meritorious, have examined and passed upon a considerable number of such claims, and have stated that they would have allowed the same for payment, but for the limitation made in the law. I would recommend that the Auditor be authorized to issue warrants in payment of such accounts as were so passed upon by the Commissioners, the same being first approved by the Governor. The accounts so passed upon are now on file in the Auditor's office.

THE PHYSICAL RESOURCES OF OUR STATE.

The physical resources of a State are the foundation of all others. They make it great or little. They shape its destiny. They even affect its moral and religious character. History teaches this truth. All the great nations of ancient and modern times demonstrate it.

—2

Egypt, Syria, Greece, Rome; Great Britain, France, the United States, are so many proofs that favorable physical situations and resources are absolutely necessary to material and moral development. Illinois, in this respect, stands pre-eminent among the States of the Union. She is the heart of the Northwest. In agricultural resources she is unsurpassed. In manufacturing and commercial facilities she has no superior. On the east, south and west, the Great River of the continent and its tributaries water her border counties, while their branches penetrate to every part of the State, irrigating her soil, draining her low lands, and affording water power for her manufactures. The Illinois river runs for over two hundred miles through the State, from northeast to southwest, forming a natural highway between the lakes and the Mississippi, the key of which is entirely in our possession. This highway is one of the most important of the physical resources of the State; while, in a military point of view, it enables us to dominate the lakes on the one hand, and the Father of Waters on the other. A State, holding this great water-way, must always be a power on the continent, as well as in the Union. Then, we have, on the northeast, an outlet to the ocean through the great lakes, those inland seas of the continent; while that one of them, Michigan, which laves our northeastern border, is almost land-locked, and thus the least liable to hostile incursions from foreign powers. This secures to us the site for a naval depot, for dock-yards, for the building and repair of vessels, for foundries for cannon, for workshops for all descriptions of war material, at some point on Lake Michigan, between the Wisconsin and Indiana State lines. Our State is also on the direct route of the Pacific railroad, which must intersect it from east to west; thus making it a portion of the great highway between Europe and the Indies. Then, again, all our lines of communication, from the interior of the State to shipping points connected with tide-water, at which bulky articles of merchandise or agricultural products can be received or delivered, are short. This saves the cost of lengthy transportation of such articles by railway, which must always be expensive. At present, in some of the States to the west and northwest of us, large quantities of grain have been stored on the navigable rivers for the last two seasons. On account of low water it cannot be sent to market by steamboat, while the cost of railway transportation would eat up its value. This can never be the case in Illinois, as long as water runs in the Mississippi, and that of the great lakes flows unobstructed to the sea. But not alone do we possess agricultural resources of an almost unlimited character: we have also within the limits of our State, facilities for manufactures, which equal those of nearly all the other States of the Union combined. Beneath the surface of our blooming prairies and beautiful woodlands are millions of tons of coal, easy of access, close to the great centers of commerce and manufactures, on great navigable rivers, and intersected by railway facilities of the best description.

Illinois, in 1860, was the fourth State in the Union in the number of tons of coal produced. But what has been produced bears no comparison to what may be. Our State Geologist assures me that in a single county in this State there are a thousand millions tons of coal awaiting the various uses to which the civilization of the future will apply it. It will thus be seen that Illinois possesses within itself the physical resources of not only a great State, but a great nation.

But if Providence has been bountiful in the natural resources of the State, it is necessary that man must be able and willing to use them to advantage; that he must have the capacity both to discern the capabilities of our situation and turn them to the advantage of our own and the people of other climes and countries. While, as I have shown, the physical resources of a State are the foundation of all other, it is also true that the people of a State must be equal to the demands and requirements of its physical capabilities. The most favored situation may be thrown away on a degenerate or incapable people. But, happily, we not only possess the physical resources of a great nation, but the mental and moral capacities of a dominant and progressive race. All it needs, then, for a proper development of our resources is, that our efforts be well directed; that we organize and direct labor, to the end that the greatest amount of development may be attained by the least possible expenditure of brute force; that by combination of effort, by organization of industry, by bringing into harmonious working development the three great branches of human industry—agriculture, manufactures and commerce—we may so weld each apparently hostile but really mutually dependent interest, into such a symmetrical whole, as to produce the most perfect social system. And this has been the aim of philosophy and statesmanship since the world began. But it can only be attained by the triumph of mind over matter; by a continual progress, in which the apparently inert forces of nature are made to subserve the highest uses of man.

The war now being waged has tended, more than any other event in the history of the country, to militate against the Jeffersonian idea, that "the best government is that which governs least." The war has not only, of necessity, given more power to, but has led to a more intimate prevision of the government over every material interest of society. By creating a large debt, it has necessitated an extended and elaborate system of taxation. This system takes note of every man's business, its profits and its probable future increase, so that the State may know what revenue it has at the present time and what it may depend on in the future. But, by creating a large debt, the war has also created a means of stimulating the industry of the country. It has created a credit, in the shape of public securities, which is so much banking capital for the industry of the nation, and forms a sure basis for creating more wealth through all the ramifications of industry. A merely agricultural country, such as the ideas of the great minds of the earlier period of the democratic party believed to be the *ultima thule* of the social state, never could sustain the immense debt which we are compelled to provide for. It is only through the enlargement of the manufacturing and commercial industries of the country that it can be borne. But through those it can be made that which the people of Great Britain proudly call theirs: "a great national blessing." It can be made to enlarge, strengthen, and place upon an enduring basis of prosperity, those great material interests of the country, which are the pride as well as the distinguishing features of every civilized nation. It will be the development of manufactures and commerce to the highest possible point, which will finally rescue the present social state from the many evils which accompany it, and usher in the millenium day of true social and political equality. While I cannot say that I desire a large national debt, yet, as we are to have it, we can console ourselves that while a large debt has its disadvantages it also has its compensatory blessings. It brings the government nearer to the individual. It makes the man recognize himself as part and parcel of the State. He supports it, and he feels that it is bound to protect him. The man who pays twenty dollars of a school tax expects that his children will receive a proper education. The manufacturer, or farmer, or merchant, or ship owner, who pays his taxes on his particular branch of industry, justly expects that that industry will be fostered and protected. It is true that a great national debt binds us more closely as a people—makes us realize the great benefits of a government, while it causes us to feel its burdens. All duty is reciprocal. "With whatever measure ye mete, it shall be measured to you again."

But it is to our debt, as a means of stimulating our industrial interests, that I particularly desire to call your attention ; because it lies in your power to provide the means through which those interests can be enlarged and extended. We must utilize the credits of the State and nation, if we would keep pace with the progress of other states and peoples; if we desire to bear our share of the burdens of the present war; if we hope when the white-winged messenger of peace shall glad a distracted country, to provide employment for the thousands of our "gallant boys in blue," who are now braving the storms of battle on many fields, when they return to the peaceful avocations of industry. We must encourage the formation of corporations for extending agriculture, manufactures and commerce. We must mobilize capital, so that it shall not be "buried in a napkin," but shall earn for itself the ability to increase, and, by such increase, stimulate industry and re-create itself. I feel deeply on this subject, because, from a careful study of the condition of our national finances, I am irresistibly led to the conclusion that, in order to pay the interest on our debt and carry on the war to a triumphant close, it is absolutely necessary that the resources of the nation should be enlarged and extended. The labor and capital of the country are the bases and sources of all its wealth. It is possible that these may be overtaxed, and thus eventually permanently contracted into narrower channels ; but it is not possible, with such vast material resources as are possessed by our favored land, that the former can ever be too widely extended or too minutely varied, or that the latter can be too greatly increased or too widely diffused. Where would our State be now, as to agricultural, manufacturing and other resources, or even military power and prestige, if the internal improvement system, of which the lamented Gov. Duncan was the able and persistent advocate, had been entirely neglected, and the Empire State of the Northwest allowed to vegetate in the imperfect condition of a merely agricultural and pastoral state ?

AGRICULTURAL, MECHANICAL AND COMMERCIAL BUREAU.

In connection with the above subject, and for the benefit of the industrial interests of the State, I would respectfully recommend the creation of an Agricultural, Mechanical and Commercial Bureau of Statistics. This would be a highly useful department of state government, as well as a great assistance to immigration. But this is but a small part of the benefit it would confer. The nation is passing into a new era of its existence. Old forms must be abandoned, and enlarged views of the principles of government accepted. The garments of the youth are too contracted for the man. With increasing and varying industrial pursuits, the people demand increased duties on the part of the State. At present, corporations, representing special interests, take upon them duties which properly belong to the State at large. Thus the only statistical tables are those prepared by the Chambers of Commerce of our cities, or by corporations interested in a special branch of industry. These tables are, of course, but partial representations of the condition of the industrial interests of the State. We should have a Bureau, which would prepare statistics and present facts regarding all the industrial interests of the State, agricultural, mechanical and commercial. These would be of use, not only to the farmer, the manufacturer and the merchant, but to the statesman and social economist. A short time since, when a distinguished foreign statesman requested to see a compilation of the social and industrial statistics of the State, it was a matter of embarrassment to me, when compelled to inform him that there was no such work in existence. Such a work would be more highly useful than most persons are apt to imagine. It would enable the merchant to regulate the quantity of his stocks, the farmer to fix his prices, the manufacturer to determine his wants, and the statesman to draw up the most comprehensive and least oppressive system of taxation. As we now stand, in this respect, all these things are done at haphazard. The consequence is, a loss of time and money, and, very often, our people are driven from certain markets and overstock others, through ignorance of the particular wants and necessities of the country, and the quantity of merchandize needed to supply them. Suppose the statistical tables of the State showed that Illinois possessed a certain quantity of corn in her cribs and store houses, would not this fact draw buyers from all parts to invest in the cheapest market, and not leave the people subject to a few monopolists? And so with other articles. The diffusion of knowledge on the state of the markets is one of the best safeguards to the great mass of the people against the chicanery and fraud of speculators, monopolists and middle-men generally. To protect the weak against the encroachments of the strong, is one of the primary objects of government. For these and other reasons, I earnestly recommend the establishment of a Bureau of Statistics, to be presided over by a Commissioner practically familiar with the great industrial interests of the State.

GEOLOGICAL SURVEY.

This work has now been in progress nearly seven years, under the charge of the present director, and his reports, embracing the results of the labors of the Geological corps employed in the survey, have been, from time to time, presented to the proper authorities for publication. A voluminous report is now ready, embracing the general result of all the labor performed up to the present time, with about fifty plates of illustration, besides the necessary maps and geological sections, which have been executed in a manner highly creditable to the artists who have been employed in this department. It is greatly to be desired that some provision should be made by the Legislature, at its present session, for the publication of this work; for, although the responsibility is thrown on the Executive, by the law organizing the survey, there is no special provision in that law for placing at my disposal the means necessary to defray the expenses attending it.

For further information in relation to the present condition of this work, I refer you to the " Report of Progress " of the State Geologist, which is herewith submitted, and to my former messages, in which this subject is more fully presented.

THE PENITENTIARY.

Since my last message, the work upon the State Penitentiary has gone on vigorously, and gratifying progress has been made. But the appropriation voted by the last Legislature for the finishing of this institution, and which, at the time, was believed to be sufficient, has been exhausted, leaving some important and necessary portions of the work still incomplete. The usual detailed reports of the officers of the penitentiary have been received by the Auditor, and will be duly submitted to the Legislature. The commissioners present a statement of the management of the institution, and of expenditures upon it during the last two years, and state its future needs. It will remain for the Legislature to do, in its wisdom, what shall be thought best to preserve and promote this great State undertaking.

As it has been charged by a portion of the press of the State that the lease of penitentiary convicts made to James M. Pittman, at the session of June, 1863, was a fraud upon the State, and that the interests of the State, as well as the discipline of the convicts, very materially suffer under the present management, I deem it my duty to recommend the General Assembly to institute a thorough investigation of the charges made, and into the management and discipline of the penitentiary. The almost complete absorption of my time by the military affairs of the State has prevented me from giving that attention to the subject of the discipline and well-being of the convicts as I, under other circumstances, should have done.

The object of punishment is not only to deprive the offender of the opportunity of committing further crime, and to deter others from its commission, but also a most important object is the reformation of the offender, especially where, after his release, he is to go back and become a member of society. After conferring with those who have had experience on this subject, I am fully satisfied that there should be, as we have at the head of our State benevolent institutions, some general superintendent of every such institution: a man of the highest moral character, of practical wisdom and business talent, who should be responsible for the entire control of the penitentiary. He should appoint the guards, clerks, stewards, and all the inferior officers; he should regulate the police, arrange the discipline, appropriate the funds for the necessary expenses, transact the business of the prison, either by agents, clerks, or contractors, and always have the control of the convicts. He should have a fixed salary, and not a per centage on the profits. Secondly, the warden should have the general care of the convicts in his charge; also, superintendence of the guards and of the police. He should not be in any way interested in the business of the prison, except to oversee the men in their labor, and discipline offenders under rules laid down by the general superintendent. He should also have a fixed salary.

A liberal appropriation should be made for the maintenance of an efficient chaplain—one who should have the moral and religious care of the men; the regulation of their religious services; should select books for the library, (for which purpose a liberal appropriation should be made;) be allowed to write letters for the convicts; and should have free access to the prisoners and the hospital. And here I must say, in most emphatic terms, that the fact that the State allows only five dollars per week to the chaplain of the State, and where there are six hundred convicts, is a disgrace to the State, which this Legislature, I trust, will wipe out, and give to the chaplain a salary of not less than one thousand dollars per year. Also, as not one dime is allowed for newspapers, I recommend that at least one hundred dollars be appropriated for newspapers, to be selected by the superintendent, and circulated among the convicts.

The province of the physician should be to administer to the infirmities of the convicts, and be responsible to the general superintendent for his care and attention.

Such, generally, in my humble opinion, should be the outline of the penitentiary management. I have no hesitation in suggesting that some such system, perfected by men of practical wisdom and experience, would result in vast saving to the State, and largely promote the welfare of the unhappy multitudes thrown upon its care, and lead to many permanent reformations of the prisoners. All the dictates of humanity require that particular attention should be given to this important subject by the members of the General Assembly. I refer you to two interesting communications from the present and former chaplains, transmitted herewith.

EDUCATION.

For a view of the progress and present condition of the common and Normal schools of the State, I refer you to the report of the Superintendent of Public Instruction, and invite your attention to the necessity of making provision for the immediate expansion and more perfect development of the system. The grand procession of events, political and military, which crowd the present, must not blind us to the inexorable demands of the future. No lesson of

—3

this historic period is being more impressively taught us than this: that under a constitution like ours the whole people must be trained to a just conception of their rights as men ; of their duties as citizens ; and of their sacred obligations as patriots. This, in theory, is the end sought by our system of free schools, and very great progress has been made. But the time has come when a vast accession must be made to the educational forces of the State. Ten years have brought us to a new era, demanding new agencies, new measures, and a more comprehensive, aggressive and liberal educational policy. More money must be appropriated, more men must be employed, more forces organized and put in operation. The progress of events has superannuated the scale of operations upon which our free school system was inaugurated. What did very well in 1855, will not do for 1865.

Much of the machinery of common schools needs to be simplified, reorganized and perfected ; temporary schools of instruction for teachers must be organized and conducted, at suitable points, throughout the State ; the changeless laws of mental growth and action must be proclaimed to the people everywhere, that they may be able to estimate the difference between right and wrong methods of teaching—the priceless blessings of good teachers and schools, and the worthlessness of bad ones ; the duty of obedience to hygienic laws in the management of schools, must be inculcated, that we may have a generation of youth sound in body as well as in mind ; a spirit of taste and beauty must be diffused until the chaste and attractive, though simple and uncostly, designs of modern improved school architecture shall be substituted for the monotonous deformity which now prevails in most of our rural districts ; in a word, the people must be led to understand the true idea and end of education itself—*why* men should be educated, and *how* they should be educated, as set forth with unanswerable power in the last biennial report, to the end that they may see the inevitable abyss into which a republican government must ultimately plunge without intelligence and virtue co-extensive with the franchises of the citizen under the constitution.

To realize these grand aims, the resources of the central educational office of the State must be increased, both in men and means. It cannot be done by the Superintendent, confined to his office, for lack of clerical help, with no traveling fund and no competen assistants. It can only be done in Illinois as it has been done in

Massachusetts and other eastern States, and as it is being done in Michigan, Wisconsin, and other western States, by a liberal appropriation for State Institutes and for the State Department of Public Instruction, that the living heralds of these great educational principles may go forth among the people. Proper legislative action is of course necessary, but if our school laws were as perfect as inspiration itself could make them, they would be powerless to achieve the desired end without the living agency of qualified, experienced men. The salary of the State Superintendent should be increased to an equality, at least, with that of the Principal of the Normal University, and he should be allowed at least two assistants, with salaries sufficient to command the very best educational experience and ability. The compensation of the head of the Normal School is not too large, and should not be reduced; but no good reason can be given why the head of the whole system should receive only three-fifths as much (which is now the fact) as the presiding officer of an institution which is but a unit in that system. A comparison of the duties and responsibilities of the two positions would justify no such disparity of compensation. Much is said about the necessity of economy in public expenditures. No man shall be before me in acting upon that principle. I advocate liberal appropriations for educational purposes *because it is the only true economy*, in the long run. No investment will prove more profitable on final settlement.

The Normal University, under its present very able administration, is more than fulfilling the most sanguine expectations of its founders and friends, and should be regarded with just pride by every citizen of the State. Its halls are literally crowded with students from all parts of the State. It is doing a great and good work. I commend it and its interests to the confidence and favor of the Legislature.

In dismissing thus briefly this great public interest, I proclaim it as my belief that no other should receive more serious attention and enlightened action at the hands of this General Assembly. The character of our future as a State and people will depend more upon the educator than the politician. It is a disgraceful fact that this great State, so matchless in all the elements of material wealth and power—so illustrious in her record of heroism and devotion to the Union—so soon to exercise, by her position and character, a controlling influence in the councils of the nation—this great State is among the most meagre and inadequate of all the free-school States of the Union in the endowment of her State Department of Education. I trust that this will be so no longer. We cannot *afford* to neglect these interests.

CONGRESSIONAL GRANT OF LANDS FOR EDUCATIONAL PURPOSES.

It will be remembered that Congress, by act approved July 2, 1862, donated to the several States, under certain conditions, public lands, or scrip for the same, in the proportion of thirty thousand acres for each senator and representative in Congress, the proceeds of the sale of which, or the land scrip to be issued therefor, is to be invested in stocks of the United States, or of the States, or some other safe stocks, yielding not less than five per cent. upon the par value of said stocks, and to constitute a perpetual fund, the interest of which is to be inviolably appropriated to the endowment, support, and maintenance of at least one college in each State, where the leading object shall be, without excluding other scientific and classical studies, and including military tactics, to teach such branches of learning as are related to agricultural and mechanic arts, in such manner as the Legislature may prescribe, in order to promote the liberal and practical education of the industrial classes in the several pursuits and professions in life; also further providing that any State which may take the benefits of the provisions of the act, shall provide, within five years of the date of such act, at least one college, as described in the act, or the grant to the State to cease, and requiring the State, by its Legislature, to express its acceptance of the provisions of the act within two years after the date of its approval. The latter provision has been carried out by the act of the last Legislature accepting the donation, but no steps were taken to carry into effect the provisions requiring the establishment of a college, and it is for you to take such action as will secure to our State the benefit of this valuable grant.

This brief synopsis of the general features of the act of Congress, will enable you to understand more fully the position which this State, by the action of the last Legislature, occupies in reference to the subject.

Pursuant to the acceptance, and after being duly notified thereof, the Secretary of the Interior has placed in my hands land scrip for the location of four hundred and eighty thousand acres. There being no public lands within the limits of this State subject to private entry, upon which said scrip can be properly located, it becomes the duty of the General Assembly to provide by law, for its sale and investment of the proceeds thereof in stocks, as contemplated and required by said act of Congress. There remains but a little more than two years within which time the State must comply with the provisions of the act, and to establish a college or colleges for the purposes specified, or the grant, as to this State, is to cease.

The shortness of the time, the importance and magnitude of the enterprise, its effects upon the educational interests of the State, and the variety of great questions involved, justify me in calling your special attention to the subject at this time. I therefore advise that a commission be appointed, charged with the duty of carrying out the provisions of the act of Congress, under such safeguards as your wisdom may suggest and approve. No part of the fund arising from this grant can be appropriated to the erection or repair of edifices or buildings, and it therefore becomes necessary for the General Assembly to provide for the same within the time limited by the act of Congress. Doubtless there are many localities within the State, which would undertake to furnish the requisite buildings and structures for such an institution without cost to the State, in consideration of the local benefits they may be supposed to derive from the same; and I, therefore, recommend that the appointment of a commission, to locate said institution, be provided for by act of the General Assembly, and that the powers and duties of said commission be so specified and defined as to insure a due consideration of the best interests of the cause of industrial education, in its relation to the whole people of the State.

At the fair of the State Agricultural Society, held during the month of September last, this subject was ably discussed, by the farmers and mechanics present, at a series of conventions called for the purpose. The views and suggestions, will be submitted to you by the committee appointed at that time, together with the draft of a bill, embodying the views of the agricultural and mechanical interests represented at said fair. The eminent qualifications of the gentlemen composing this committee, for determining what would be to the best educational interests of the mechanical and agricultural classes, as well as the respectable and prominent standing which they occupy in society, entitle their recommendations to your most favorable consideration. A committee, also representing the views of the mechanics of Chicago, will lay a communication before you, which, with any other communications on the subject, will, I trust, receive your careful consideration.

It is needless for me to add, that to this General Assembly is committed this great and sacred trust, in which not alone the present, but future generations of this State are deeply interested. If it is economically and wisely administered, it will be a source of great blessings, and will reflect credit upon this General Assembly, upon whom has devolved the important responsibility of devising the best mode for carrying out the great purposes of its creation. There are other features of said act of Congress which should be responded to by legislation on the part of the General Assembly, but which need not be enumerated. The whole subject, freighted as it is with the most important hopes and promises for the future of our young and growing State, I leave in your hands, trusting that in whatever may be done, the rights of the farmers and mechanics, for whose benefit this munificent donation was made, will be fully regarded.

A REGISTRY LAW.

The elective franchise is a distinguishing feature of our republican system. The legislation of the country, its policy and its institutions, are determined by the majority of the legal voters of the state or nation, and the mode of ascertaining that majority is by the ballots of the voters deposited in the ballot box. In the absence of any guards or restrictions thrown around the ballot box, a fair expression of the will of the majority may be defeated by illegal voting. It is but too often the case that corrupting influences are brought to bear upon voters who, from mercenary considerations, or under political excitement, are led to vote oftener than they are entitled, and who lack the requirements of age, residence, or other qualifications required by the constitution and laws. It is sometimes the case that men who plead exemption from military service, and claim the protection of foreign governments in case of a draft, are yet among the first to claim and exercise the right of suffrage at the polls. Again, instances are known of unworthy citizens who go from place to place, casting their votes under assumed names, wherever, through the oversight or political connivance of the judges of the election, they can have them received. To prevent such practices, I recommend the passage of a stringent registry law, requiring the name of each voter to be recorded for a given number of days previous to such general election. The time should be sufficient to secure an investigation into the qualifications of the voter in every doubtful case. Laws of this character have been found to operate well and meet the approbation of men of all parties who desire to maintain the purity of the ballot box.

BLACK LAWS.

Of the black laws I have but little to say, except to recommend that you sweep them from the statute book with a swift, relentless hand. My opinion of them cannot be better expressed than in the language of a resolution, which as a member of the General Assembly in February, 1849, I had the honor in a feeble minority to advocate, "declaring the laws of the State, applicable to negroes and mulattoes, tyrannical, iniquitous and oppressive upon this weak, harmless and unfortunate class, and unbecoming the statutes of a free, magnanimous, enlightened and christian nation." They were originally enacted to gratify an unjustifiable public prejudice against the friends of liberty, and an inhuman feeling towards a poor, unfortunate class of our fellow citizens. They assumed a fact, which, to the honor of the Jeffersonian ordinance of 1787, never existed, that slavery did or could exist in the free state of Illinois. Section 9 of these laws provides that "if any slave or servant shall be found ten miles from the tenement of his or her master 'without a pass,' he may be punished with stripes not exceeding thirty-five"—thus by the phraseology of the law recognizing the existence of the institution of slavery within our borders and prescribing an infamous punishment. It is unconstitutional, as decided by the Supreme Court in this State, "in attempting to legislate upon the subject of the rendition of fugitive slaves to their masters, over which subject the court decides that Congress has supreme and exclusive power." It authorizes a system of slavery, by providing that every colored man who shall be found in this State "without having *a certificate of freedom,*" shall be deemed a runaway *slave or servant*—"to be committed to the custody of the sheriff of the county, who shall advertise him at the court house door," and "to hire him out for the best price he can get," "from month to month," "for the space of one year." Any law, thus placing any man, white or black, in the power of a purchaser, for money, is utterly inconsistent with the humanity of the age and the spirit of our free constitution. These laws are unconstitutional, because by the laws of many of our States free colored persons are citizens, and the constitution of the United States expressly provides that "the citizens of each State shall be entitled to all the privileges of citizens in the several States."

An examination of the various provisions of these laws will satisfy this General Assembly of their inhumanity, and the humane and philanthropic will everywhere hail their repeal with joyful acclamations.

In reply to those who say that if these laws are repealed we shall have a large influx of free negroes into this State, I have to answer that the laws are now almost a dead letter. Negroes are not kept out of the State by them, for it is only now and then, indeed a rare case, that a man can be found who is barbarian enough to insist upon the application of the penalties imposed by these laws. And upon the subject I cannot present my views better than by the following extract from my message of January 5th 1863. Referring to the emancipation policy of the administration, I say :

"I am sure of two things : First—that when slavery is removed, this rebellion will die out, and not before. Second—I believe and predict, and commit the prediction in this State paper to meet the verdict of my successors in office and of posterity, that the change brought about by the policy of emancipation will pass off in a way *so quietly and so easily,* that the world will stand amazed that we should have entertained such fears of its evils. During the war, there will be necessarily some suffering among so many slaves thrown out of employment, and many, perhaps large numbers of them, will seek a temporary refuge in the free states, and every man who has a human heart within him, will treat them kindly ; but with the return of peace, the demand for labor in the south will be greatly increased, and there will be an exodus not only of these fugitives, but of the free colored population to the south. The demand for labor in the south will be greatly increased by the subdivision of large farms into numerous small ones, in the hands of a much larger number of owners; also by the reclamation of immense regions of fertile country in all our southern states, waiting only the plastic touch of free labor, the settlement of which has been retarded by the existence of slavery, tending, as it always has, and necessarily always will, to discourage the immigration of free white citizens. No reasonable fears of competition with the free labor of the northern states need be entertained, because the emancipated slave will have protection and employment upon the soil which he has heretofore cultivated in bondage. Emancipation does not increase the number of negroes by an additional one. There will not be a single acre of land less for cultivation, but a great deal more will probably be cultivated; there will be the same and an increasing demand for the culture of cotton, tobacco, sugar, and rice, for which the negro is peculiarly adapted; the southern climate will remain unchanged, congenial to his constitution; and it is in the highest degree improbable that the negro will leave the state of his nativity, where his labor is in demand, where he understands, better than any one else, the business to be done, and where the climate is adapted to him, to seek the cold climates of the north, to face the strong competition of northern, skilled free-labor, to encounter the preju dice against his color, and the pauperism and neglect which would meet him on every hand."

I will not say that legislation will not be necessary upon this subject of the residence of free negroes in our midst ; but I will say, that whatever is necessary should be free from political prejudice, having regard to the welfare of our own, free, white citizens, and, at the same time, marked with humanity and a due regard to that unfortunate class of our fellow beings whom Providence, in its wise and inscrutible plans, has placed in our care.

SOLDIERS' VOTING.

In my last message I recommended, in strong terms, the importance and justice of an enactment extending to our citizen soldiers, in the field, the right of suffrage, but no action was had upon the same. During the last two years the subject has been fully considered and acted upon in many of the loyal States, and although the constitutions of the States have been framed without reference to a state of war, yet the subject has undergone the scrutiny of the highest judicial tribunals, and the right to take the votes of soldiers in the field has been clearly recognized. Laws passed for this purpose have been carried into operation and found to operate well, without any public injury. I can see nothing in our State constitution which prohibits the passage of such a law. Section 1, Art. 6 of our State constitution, provides as follows: "In all elections, every white male citizen, above the age of twenty-one years, having resided in the State one year next preceding any election, shall be entitled to vote at such election ; and every white male inhabitant, of the age aforesaid, who may be a resident at the time of the adoption of this constitution, shall have the right of voting as aforesaid ; but no such citizen or inhabitant shall be entitled to vote, except in the district or county in which he shall actually reside at the time of such election." It is evident, from this clause, that the elector cannot vote in any other precinct than that in which he actually resides.

Section 4, Art. 6 of the constitution of the United States, provides that "No elector shall be deemed to have lost his residence in this State by reason of his absence on the business of the United States or of this State."

Under this latter clause, a minister of the United States to a foreign court, though absent for years, is an actual resident of the district or county in which he resided at the time he left the country, on his mission. The same may be said of the soldier who has left the county or district, because he is absent on the business of the United States, and therefore does not lose his residence. Now, is it reasonable to presume that the framers of our constitution, while thus preserving the residence of the soldier, evidently for the purpose of securing to him the right of suffrage, at the same time meant to prohibit the Legislature from making any provision to enable him to exercise that right ? While the elector is required "to vote in the district or county" in which he resides, it is not necessarily required that he is to be present, in person, at the polls, and cast his vote. The object of the framers of the constitution was to preserve the purity of the ballot box, and to prevent the voter from voting more than once, or at more places than one, at the same election. The object evidently was, to provide that his vote should only be cast in the one district or county in which he resided. Now the constitution, and the object of its framers, are fully complied with, when the soldier has cast his vote in his district or county, whether he be present, and cast his vote there in person, or whether the ballot is deposited there by his attorney, under the proper checks and restrictions—as to his qualifications of age, residence, etc.—or whether his vote is taken in the field, in some mode to be provided by the Legislature, and deposited in the ballot box of the district or county in which he resides, as has been provided in the laws of several of the States. The following plan, with such guards and details as will prevent frauds, is suggested, as a practicable way of effecting the object: The three field officers, or, in their absence, the three ranking officers of each regiment of infantry or cavalry, and three highest commissioned officers, or those acting in their places, of each battery of artillery, or each company or squadron of infantry or cavalry on detached service, might be made the inspectors of the election, with power to appoint the proper person clerk of the election, so that the vote may be taken on the day fixed by the constitution.

There is no way of reaching the case by amendment to the constitution, without disfranchising the soldier for at least two years to come, for the constitution requires that two-thirds of the General Assembly shall recommend to the people to vote for or against calling a convention to amend the constitution, at the next regular election of members of the General Assembly, and that the General Assembly thus elected shall, within three months, call an election for members to the convention. It would require a still longer time to reach the object under the clause which provides for amendment by submitting it as a single proposition. It is therefore plain that if this General Assembly fails to pass a law authorizing our soldiers to vote, these gallant defenders of our homes and liberties must be disfranchised for over two years to come.

I recommend therefore to you, as one of your first acts, the passage of a law providing for taking the votes of our soldiers in the field. Indeed, I will say, decorously however, that failure to protect the rights of the noble men who have left business and property, home and kindred, to preserve to you the enjoyment of this same peaceful right of suffrage, together with all other rights you hold dear, would subject you to the charge of being unfaithful servants to your country. The soldiers are citizens; they are the people of the country; their persons, their families, their property, their rights are as deeply affected by the legislation of the country as those of the citizens who remain at home, in the quiet enjoyment of peace and safety. If the soldier is not worthy to vote, who is? If he who bares his breast to the storm of battle, and bears aloft our flag, against the hordes who are madly striving to tear down our magnificent temple of constitutional liberty; if he shall have no voice in selecting his rulers, who shall? Therefore let this General Assembly signalize its patriotism by this act of prompt and necessary justice to the gallant citizen soldier of the State.

I would suggest to the General Assembly that, while I do not anticipate an unfavorable decision of the Supreme Court upon an enactment to be passed securing the right of suffrage to the soldiers, yet, in view of any such contingency, proper action should be taken for amendment to the constitution, as the next only mode of securing the object.

WAR RECORD OF ILLINOIS.

CONDUCT OF THE WAR.

Appreciating, before the first gun was fired at Sumter, the determination of treasonable political leaders to inaugurate rebellion, and, when war was actually made against the government, the great preparation made by them for revolt, and the magnitude of the struggle we would be compelled to pass through, I earnestly insisted upon and urged more extensive preparation for the prosecution of the war. The conciliatory policy which looked towards avoiding a bitter struggle, by appeals to the loyal sentiment of the southern States, and the justification in the ultimate rigid prosecution of war, should that fail; thus placing the government in a consistent and peaceful attitude toward foreign nations, and establishing, by long forbearance, the disposition of one section, it the majority and in power, to concede and allay the animosities of the other section, in the minority, and defeated at the ballot-box; also, that if the struggle endangered the existence of the government and Union under our old constitution, that the President, as commander-in-chief of the armies and navy of the Republic, would be justified by the civilized world, and by the trust reposed in him, in waging war, even to the destruction of institutions which endangered the peace of all other nations, and which foreign powers admit, and the majority of our own people had declared, as subversive of the constitution, and dangerous to the existence of the Union. These views are perhaps sound in theory, and may ultimately redound to our credit in historic pages; but I never altogether sympathized with the policy. The events of the war, and revolutions in public sentiment, have sustained the warnings given in the early days of open treason, and my position taken at the firs declaration of secession and war : "*that secession was disunion;* that to concede to one State the right to release her people from the duties and obligations belonging to their citizenship, and you would, by that act, annihilate the sovereignty of the Union, by prostrating its ability to secure allegiance ;" also, that the violation of law, and a defiance of the authority and power of the General Government, however small, demanded the immediate punishment of the offenders, and the complete vindication of national integrity ; and that the President should immediately employ the *whole material of the government, moral, political and physical,* if need be, to preserve, protect and defend the constitution of the United States.

After the war had progressed a year, and the mild measures which were still persistently advocated by many friends of the administration, and with all the evidence, on the part of the rebels, for complete preparation and determination to wage a long and desperate war against the government, I sent the President the following dispatch :

EXECUTIVE DEPARTMENT, SPRINGFIELD, ILLINOIS, *July* 11*th*, 1862.

President Lincoln, Washington, D. C.:

The crisis of the war and our national existence is upon us. The time has come for the adoption of more decisive measures. Greater vigor and earnestness must be infused into our military movements. Blows must be struck at the vital parts of the rebellion. The government should employ every available means compatible with the rules of warfare to subject the traitors. Summon to the standard of the Republic all men willing to fight for the Union. Let loyalty, and that alone, be the dividing line between the nation and its foes. Generals should not be permitted to fritter away the sinews of our brave men in guarding the property of traitors, and in driving back into their hands loyal blacks, who offer us their labor, and seek shelter beneath the federal flag. Shall we sit supinely by, and see the war sweep off the youth and strength of the land, and refuse aid from that class of men, who are at least worthy foes of traitors and the murderers of our government and of our children?

Our armies should be directed to forage on the enemy, and to cease paying traitors and their abettors exorbitant exactions for food needed by the sick or hungry soldier. Mild and conciliatory means have been tried in vain to recall the rebels to their allegiance. The conservative policy has utterly failed to reduce traitors to obedience, and to restore the supremacy of the laws. They have, by means of sweeping conscriptions, gathered in countless hordes, and threaten to beat back and overwhelm the armies of the Union. With blood and treason in their hearts, they flaunt the black flag of rebellion in the face of the government, and threaten to butcher our brave and loyal armies with foreign bayonets. They arm negroes and merciless savages in their behalf.

Mr. Lincoln, the crisis demands greater and sterner measures. Proclaim anew the good old motto of the Republic, "Liberty and Union, now and forever, one and inseparable," and accept the services of *all loyal men*, and it will be in your power to stamp armies out of the earth—irresistible armies, that will bear our banners to certain victory.

In any event, Illinois, already alive with ... at of drum, and resounding with the tramp of new recruits, will respond to your call. Adopt this policy, and she will leap like a flaming giant into the fight.

This policy for the conduct of the war will render foreign intervention impossible, and the arms of the Republic invincible. It will bring the conflict to a speedy close, and secure peace on a permanent basis.

RICHARD YATES,
Governor of Illinois.

Impressed with these views, and the necessity of each State giving immediate and the most practical support to the government, and inspired by the unparalleled enthusiasm of the people of Illinois, I asked that millions should be armed where the government asked, in limited calls, only for a few hundred thousand men. Bull Run, Carthage, Wilson's Creek, and the attitude of Kentucky and Missouri, painfully demonstrated the inadequacy of preparation on the part of the government for the crisis; and had it not been for the overpowering uprising of the people of the free States, and their loyal and determined expression to take the war in their own hands, we might have had enacted on our own soil the scenes which have desolated border States, and the country involved in a strife for a period and in bitterness far exceeding the darkest periods we have passed in the last three years.

Before the battle of Bull Run, and before important points being occupied by rebel troops—after consultation with the Governors of the loyal States, and with distinguished citizens of Illinois, who, as commanding generals, have led our gallant soldiers to brilliant victories—I recommended the occupation of New Orleans, Memphis, Columbus, and commanding positions on the Cumberland and Tennessee rivers, by United States regular troops; thus obviating the necessity of arraying sections against each other by the employment of a volunteer army, and plainly foreshadowing the determination of the government to firmly resist and punish violations of law, and overwhelm the presumptuous insolence of rebel leaders in the act of inaugurating rebellion in the States. These efforts were unavailing; and the government was afterward compelled to occupy these important positions by larger armies of volunteer troops, and at fearful sacrifice of life, and expenditure of millions of dollars. The conciliatory policy, so destructive to our interests in the west, entered largely into the organization of the army formed for the defense of the national capital, and offensive operations in Virginia; and we had the lamentable picture of the General chosen to chief command issuing orders that slaves discovered in making war for the government against their rebellious masters should be put down with an iron hand, and one temporizing Governor of Missouri pronouncing the act of the President, in calling for a detachment of militia to enforce the national authority, "illegal, unconstitutional, revolutionary, inhuman, diabolical, and cannot be complied with." Another replied that "Kentucky will furnish no troops for the wicked purpose of subduing her sister southern States;" and "Tennessee will not furnish a single man for coercion."

Kid glove in civil council, and kid glove and warm sympathy "for our erring southern brethren" in the organization of the eastern army, made service there distasteful to western volunteers; and this sentiment impressed me with the importance of securing the close consolidation of our State forces at the commencement of the war; and, as far as it was consistent or possible for me to do so, I secured the intimate association of all our regiments in brigade and division organizations in the field. This also facilitated the convenient distribution of supplies then issued by the State for the General Government; provided the earliest relief possible to the largest number, after long marches and severe engagements; afforded the easiest and cheapest transit of sanitary supplies to field and general hospitals; and concentrated our contingents to the na_tional army in corps designed for campaigns through territory famil. iar to both officers and men, and in which they would more speedily develop their genius for military life, and render the most efficient and practical service to the government. It was natural to presume that our young men who passed their early days in States south of the Ohio, and deplored the dedication of their old homesteads and associations to the cause of rebellion; and that the immigrant from New England, the Middle States, and Europe, dwelling upon our fertile prairies, and growing rich and independent from the products of free labor, would recognize the importance and more zealously prosecute the re-conquest of the valley of the Mississippi, and the control of its great river—our natural outlet to the ocean, so vital to the success of our enemies, and so necessary to the protection of our local interests, and the integrity of the Union—and that our whole people would sympathize with and sustain efforts to thus gather and unite the whole strength of the State in solid force against treason, and for the restoration of the national unity, perfect in all its parts.

Belmont, Donelson, Island No. 10, Shiloh, Corinth, Parker s Cross Roads, Port Gibson, Raymond, Champion Hills, Black River, Siege of Vicksburg, Perryville, Stone River, Chickamauga, Lookout Mountain, Atlanta, Franklin, Nashville, and the triumphal march of Sherman, speak in thunder tones of the consolidated efforts of Illinois, vieing with the volunteers of other States in battling for the Union.

We have lost thousands of our best men, and whole regiments and batteries, in the conflicts of this fearful war: but we have not to deplore the decimation of the ranks of gallant regiments, led by timid and halting generals on fruitless and purposeless campaigns, prosecuted without skill or vigor, and with the deplorable *morale* of a fear to punish traitors not actually in arms, and the employment of the best strength of their armies in protecting rebel property.

The following exhibits the quotas of the State under respective calls since commencement of the war, and the number of men furnished to the national armies to the present time :

Our quota, under calls of the President

In 1861, was 47,785
In 1862, "   32,685
In 1863, "   64,630
In 1864, "   52,260

Total quotas under all calls prior to Dec. 1, 1864.....197,360

During the years 1861, 1862, and to the 18th day of October, 1863, the State, by voluntary enlistment, had exceeded its quota under all calls. Prior to that date settlements had not been made with the War Department, because of the voluntary action of our people in meeting the requirements of the country and their persistence in organizing, with unparalleled enthusiasm and determination, a larger number of regiments and batteries than the actual quotas under each levy called for. Prior to 17th October, 1863, the State had furnished and been credited with one hundred and twenty-five thousand three hundred and twenty-one (125,321) men —a surplus of eight thousand one hundred and fifty-one (8,151) over all other calls, to be credited to our quota for that call, and which reduced it to 19,779 men ; and we claimed, besides, other credits, which could not be fully adjusted because of imperfect record of citizens (and in some cases whole companies of Illinoisans) who had entered the service in regiments of other States, at times when our quotas on special calls were full, and because of which I was compelled to decline their services. Six thousand and thirty, two (6,032) citizens of Illinois prior to that date had been enlisted in Missouri regiments, and residents of Missouri had enlisted and been mustered in Illinois regiments, which left a credit, as between the States, in favor of Illinois of 4,373 men.

After adjustment of credit of 125,321, at and prior to October, 1863, it was ascertained we were entitled to an additional credit of 10,947, which increased the number enrolled *in our own regiments*, and for which we were entitled to credit prior to that call, to 136,-268—leaving the whole account, at that date, thus:

```
Quotas under all calls to October, 1863............... 145,100
Credits for enlistments in Illinois regiments......136,268
Balance in Missouri regiments................   4,373
                                                         ———— 140,641
Balance due the government......................   4,459
```

At this time there was a claim made by the State for volunteers previously furnished, which would more than account for the balance against us of 4,459. This adjustment was made in February, 1864, and was *exclusive of old regiments re-enlisting as veterans*, and disclosed the fact that at the time the first draft was ordered, viz: January 1st, 1864, under the call of October, 1863, Illinois had exceeded her quota, and, by the voluntarily demonstrated patriotism of her people, was free from draft.

The unadjusted balances of the State claimed as above were allowed in the settlement made with the War Department, in August last.

Between the first day of October, 1863, and the first day of December, 1864, we have furnished and received additional credits for fifty-five thousand six hundred and nineteen (55,619) men which, added to credit of 140,641 to October 1, 1863, makes 197,-260 men, which leaves our whole account thus:

```
Quotas of the State under all calls prior to Dec. 1, 1864...197,360
Total credits for three years volunteers, drafted men and
  substitutes to Dec. 1, 1864........................197,260
                                                          ————
Balance due the government Dec. 1, 1864............   100
```
—4

The deficit of *one hundred men* has been more than balanced by enlistments during the month of December, 1864.

Of the entire quota of one hundred and ninety-seven thousand three hundred and sixty (197,360) men, we have furnished *one hundred and ninety-four thousand one hundred and ninety-eight* (194,198) *volunteers* and *three thousand and sixty-two* (3,062) *drafted men*—organized as follows:

138 regiments and one battalion of infantry.
17 regiments of cavalry.
2 regiments and 8 batteries of artillery.

ONE HUNDRED DAY TROOPS.

In addition to the foregoing the State has furnished thirteen (13) regiments and two companies of one hundred day volunteers, the following being the numerical designation, name of commanding officer and strength of each:

No. of regiment.	Commanding Officer.	Aggregate
132	Col. Thomas J. Pickett.............................	853
133	" Thaddeus Phillips...........................	851
134	" Walter W. McChesney..............................	878
135	" John S. Wolfe.......................................	855
136	" Frederick A. Johns....	842
137	" John Wood.......................................	849
138	" John W. Goodwin.......................................	835
139	" Peter Davidson.......................................	878
140	" Lorenzo H. Whitney.................................	871
141	" Stephen Bronson	842
142	" Rollin V. Ankney.................................	851
143	" Dudley C. Smith....	865
145	" George W. Lackey.................................	877
....	Capt. Simon J. Stookey, (Alton battalion—two companies).....	181
	Total	11,328

After the fall of Vicksburg, in 1863, and General Sherman's raid into Mississippi, Georgia and Alabama, active military operations were transferred from the Mississippi to Eastern Tennessee and Georgia. The forces of the enemy, during the winter of 1863-4, were being largely increased and carefully prepared for a desperate spring and summer campaign, east and west, and in April he had concentrated his strength for offensive operations in Virginia and Georgia, or, in the event of our advance, for the most determined and bitter resistance. To hold the vast extent of country wrested from the enemy, embracing many States and territories, many thousand miles of sea coast, the whole length of the Mississippi, and most of her tributaries, and protect our long lines of sea and river coast and rail communication, required an immense stationary force.

The towns and cities surrounding strongholds, posts and garrisons, situated in the midst of a doubtful and in most part disloyal population, required too great a portion of our large army for their protection and defense. In view of these circumstances, and of the palpable evidence which surrounded us that the battles about to be fought in Virginia by the army under direct supervision of Lieutenant-General Grant, and in Georgia under General Sherman, would doubtless decide the fate of the country, the Governors of the Northwestern States believed that the efficiency of the army and the prospects of crowning victories to the national arms would be greatly increased by a volunteer force, immediately raised, and which should occupy the points already taken and relieve our veteran troops, and send them forward to join the main army soon to engage the effective forces of the enemy. I therefore, in connection with Governors Brough of Ohio, Morton of Indiana, and Stone of Iowa, offered the President infantry troops for one hundred days' service, to be organized under regulations of the War Department, and to be clothed, equipped, armed, subsisted, transported and paid as other United States infantry volunteers, and to serve in fortifications wherever their services might be required, within or without the State. There being no law authorizing it, no bounty could be paid or the service credited on any draft. Our quota offered was 20,000 men, which was a fair proportion to the aggregate number (85,000) to be made up by all of said States.

Our regiments, under this call, performed indispensable and invaluable services in Kentucky, Tennessee and Missouri, relieving garrisons of veteran troops, who were sent to the front, took part in the Atlanta campaign, several of them, also composing a part of that glorious army that has penetrated the very vitals of the rebellion, and plucked some of the brightest laurels that this heroic age has woven for the patriot soldier. Five of our one hundred days regiments, after their turn of service had expired, voluntarily extended their engagement with the government, and marched to the relief of the gallant and able Rosecrans, who, at the head of an inadequate and poorly appointed army, was contending against fearful odds for the preservation of St. Louis and the safety of Missouri. The officers and soldiers of these regiments evinced the highest soldierly qualities, and fully sustained the proud record our veterans have ever maintained in the field—and the State and country owe them lasting gratitude, and we have, in a great degree, to attribute our successes in Virginia and Georgia to the timely organization and efficient services of the one hundred day volunteers, furnished by all of said States. The President has, by order, returned them the thanks of the government and the nation for the service thus rendered, and accords the full measure of praise to them, as our supporters and defenders in the rear, to which the regular reserve force of large armies are always entitled.

RECRUITING SERVICE.

The General Government has aimed to divide the burden of supplying troops for the national army equally between the loyal States, and, according to the best information attainable, I believe the States have responded fully. To husband the resources of the State, in its number of arms-bearing men, I have thrown every guard possible around the recruiting system. In 1861, by proclamation, issued in July, I forbade the recruitment of volunteers in Illinois for the regiments of other States, and discouraged our citizens from leaving the State to join the organizations of others—but in that year was partially unsuccessful, because of the small number of regiments accepted in proportion to the very large number of our citizens who tendered their services. Diligent efforts were made to trace out organizations and individuals who left the State under these circumstances, and the records in the Adjutant General's office exhibit our success in reclaiming several whole regiments, and nearly 10,000 men, distributed through various regiments of Missouri and other sister States.

In 1861 and 1862 a few arrests were made for violation of the order, and parties guilty, upon surrendering the recruits, were dismissed, upon obligation to observe the prohibition in future. In 1863 there was no marked violation of the regulation; but, in 1864, when the emergencies and casualties of the service demanded the reinforcement and large increase of the army, many of the States became almost exhausted in number of citizens who could voluntarily offer their services to the country ; and, to protect their agricul. tural, manufacturing and other industrial interests, their legisla. tures had provided, by law, for the payment of large bounties, from their State treasuries, and authorized towns and counties also to pay bounties, and to levy a tax to provide for the same—thus affording additional inducements (to residents of other States, not making such provisions,) to the general bounty and premium provided by laws of Congress.

The enrollment act of last Congress also provided for enlistment of volunteer recruits in insurrectionary districts, and provided for the appointment, by Governors of the respective States, of agents to recruit there, at State expense, and that volunteers, thus enlisted, should be credited to the quota of the town, township, ward of a city, precinct, or election district of a county procuring them.

As there was no State law for, or appropriation made, from which to pay the expenses of this system, I was unable to employ agents to recruit for the State; but in my proclamation of August 9th, 1864, announcing the quotas and credits to July 18th, 1864, and calling upon the people to fill our quota by volunteering, this system was fully presented, and towns, cities and districts invited, at their own expense, to avail themselves of the privileges of the law and orders of the war department, made in pursuance thereof, to meet delinquencies of past calls, or to fill up their quotas under call of July 18th, 1864, then pending. A very small number had agents appointed, but, I believe, without practical results—the inducements they were enabled to offer being inferior to those presented by agents of other States.

To provide against the enlistment of citizens of this State, or persons, white and colored, who had taken refuge here from States or districts in rebellion, in the regiments, or to be used as the contribution of wealthy counties or localities of other States, which would result in increasing the burdens of war (either in *men* or *dollars*) upon our citizens, I deemed it proper to issue the following proclamation :

EXECUTIVE OFFICE, }
Springfield, Illinois, August 6, 1864. }

It is hereby ordered that no recruiting for companies or regiments of other States shall be permitted in this State.

All recruiting officers or agents for other States, and the agent or attorneys of companies organized to procure substitutes for persons drafted in other States, are hereby peremptorily forbidden to recruit or enlist volunteers or substitutes within this State during the war.

This order shall apply to all residents or citizens of Illinois, as well as the citizens of other States, recruiting within this State for regiments of other States.

All recruiting agents for Illinois regiments, Provost Marshals, and loyal citizens are requested to give notice of any violation of this order, that offenders may be arrested and punished, and the objects designed by this limitation to recruiting entirely accomplished.

Illinois has heretofore promptly responded to all calls for volunteers, and it behooves every good citizen to contribute every reasonable influence to sustain our veteran regiments, which have so honored the State in efforts to sustain the Union, and I earnestly entreat all citizens who desire to enter the military service of the country to join Illinois regiments only. As our brave boys have struggled to give our State its proud position, let us eschew all selfish inducements (presented by other States) and generously sustain them and our veteran organizations in the field.

RICHARD YATES, *Governor.*

Besides enforcing the view that the State should not be called upon or allowed to furnish more than her quota, I was impelled to insist upon her husbanding our resources for the future demands of the country; also by a desire to have our entire quota assigned to our old regiments, that they might, without consolidation, retain their names and organizations —rendered illustrious by gallant deeds on scores of battle fields—and in justice to tried officers, who could not be promoted until their companies and regiments were full; and because of the immediate effectiveness of new recruits, in veteran organizations, under experienced officers. I am glad to state that the Secretary of War issued orders to the United States officers, on duty in this State, to enforce the provisions of the order.

In prompt support of the government at home, and in response to calls for troops, the State stands pre-eminently in the lead among her loyal sisters; and every click of the telegraph heralds the perseverance of Illinois Generals and the indomitable courage and bravery of Illinois sons, in every engagement of the war. Our State has furnished a very large contingent to the fighting strength of our National army. In the west, the history of the war is brilliant with recitations of the skill and prowess of our general, field, staff and line officers, and hundreds of Illinois boys in the ranks are specially singled out and commended by Generals Grant, Sherman, and other Generals of this and other States, for their noble deeds and manly daring on hotly contested fields.

One gallant Illinois boy is mentioned as being the first to plant the stars and stripes at Donelson; another, at a critical moment, anticipates the commands of a superior officer, in hurrying forward an ammunition train, and supervising hand grenades, by cutting short the fuses of heavy shell, and hurling them, with his own hands, in front of an assaulting column, into a strong redoubt at Vicksburg; and the files of my office and those of the Adjutant General are full of letters mentioning for promotion hundreds of private soldiers, who have, on every field of the war, distinguished themselves by personal gallantry, at trying and critical periods. The list of promotions from the field and staff of our regiments to Lieutenant and Major Generals, for gallant conduct and the prerequisites for efficient and successful command, compare brilliantly with the names supplied by all other States, and is positive proof of the wisdom of the Government in conferring honors and responsibilities; and the patient, vigilant and tenacious record made by our veteran regiments, in the camp, on the march and in the field, is made a subject of praise by the whole country, and will be the theme for poets and historians of all lands, for all time.

Prominent among the many distinguished names who have borne their early commissions from Illinois, I refer, with special pride, to the character and priceless services to the country of Ulysses S. Grant. In April, 1861, he tendered his personal services to me, saying "that he had been the recipient of a military education at West Point, and that now, when the country was involved in a war for its preservation and safety, he thought it his duty to offer his services in defense of the Union, and that he would esteem it a privilege to be assigned to any position where he could be useful." The plain, straight forward demeanor of the man, and the modesty and earnestness which characterized his offer of assistance, at once awakened a lively interest in him, and impressed me with a desire to secure his counsel for the benefit of volunteer organizations then forming for government service. At first, I assigned him a desk in the Executive office; and his familiarity with military organization and regulations made him an invaluable assistant in my own and the office of the Adjutant General. Soon his admirable qualities as a military commander became apparent, and I assigned him to command of the camps of organization at "Camp Yates," Springfield, "Camp Grant," Mattoon, and "Camp Douglas," at Anna, Union county, at which the 7th, 8th, 9th, 10th,

11th, 12th, 18th, 19th and 21st regiments of Illinois volunteers, raised under the call of the President, of the 15th of April, and under the "Ten Regiment Bill," of the extraordinary session of the Legislature, convened April 23d, 1861, were rendezvoused. His employment had special reference to the organization and muster of these forces—the first six into United States, and the last three into the State service. This was accomplished about the tenth day of May, 1861, at which time he left the State for a brief period, on a visit to his father, at Covington, Kentucky.

The 21st regiment of Illinois volunteers, raised in Macon, Cumberland, Piatt, Douglas, Moultrie, Edgar, Clay, Clark, Crawford and Jasper counties, for thirty-day State service, organized at the camp at Mattoon, preparatory to three years' service for the government, had become very much demoralized, under the thirty days' experiment, and doubts arose in relation to their acceptance for a longer period. I was much perplexed to find an efficient and experienced officer to take command of the regiment and take it into the three years' service. I ordered the regiment to Camp Yates, and after consulting Hon. Jesse K. Dubois, who had many friends in the regiment, and Col. John S. Loomis, Assistant Adjutant General, who was at the time in charge of the Adjutant General's office, and on terms of personal intimacy with Grant, I decided to offer the command to him, and accordingly telegraphed Captain Grant, at Covington, Kentucky, tendering him the Colonelcy. He immediately reported, accepting the commission, taking rank as Colonel of that regiment from the 15th day of June, 1861. Thirty days previous to that time the regiment numbered over one thousand men, but in consequence of laxity in discipline of the first commanding officer, and other discouraging obstacles connected with the acceptance of troops at that time, but six hundred and three men were found willing to enter the three years' service. In less than ten days Col. Grant filled the regiment to the maximum standard, and brought it to a state of discipline seldom attained in the volunteer service, in so short a time. His was the only regiment that left the camp of organization on foot. He marched from Springfield to the Illinois river, but, in an emergency requiring troops to operate against Missouri rebels, the regiment was transported by rail to Quincy, and Col. Grant was assigned to command for the protection of the Quincy and Palmyra, and Hannibal and St. Joseph railroads. He soon distinguished himself as a regimental commander, in the field, and his claims for increased rank were recognized by his friends in Springfield, and his promotion insisted upon, before his merits and services were fairly understood at Washington. His promotion was made upon the ground of his military education, fifteen years' services as a Lieutenant and Captain in the regular army, (during which time he was distinguished in the Mexican war,) his great success in organizing and disciplining his regiment, and for his energetic and vigorous prosecution of the campaign in North Missouri, and the earnestness with which he entered into the great work of waging war against the traitorous enemies of his country. His first great battle was at Belmont, an engagement which became necessary to protect our Southwestern army in Missouri from overwhelming forces being rapidly consolidated against it from Arkansas, Tennessee and Columbus, Kentucky. The struggle was a desperate one, but the tenacity and soldierly qualities of Grant and his invincible little army, gave us the first practical victory in the west. The balance of his shining record is indelibly written in the history of Henry, Donelson, Shiloh, Corinth, Vicksburg. Chattanooga, The Wilderness, siege of Richmond, and the intricate and difficult command as Lieutenant General of the armies of the Union—written in the blood and sacrifices of the heroic braves who have fallen, following him to glorious victory—written upon the hearts and memories of the loyal millions who are at the hearth-stones of our gallant and unconquerable "Boys in Blue." The impress of his genius stamps our armies, from one end of the Republic to the other; and the secret of his success in executing his plans, is in the love, enthusiasm and confidence he inspires in the soldier in the ranks, the harmony and respect of his subordinate officers, his own respect for and deference to the wishes and commands of the President, and his sympathy with the government in its war policy.

As evidence of the materials of the State of Illinois for war purposes, at the beginning of the war, and a pleasing incident of Grant's career, I refer to an article in a Vicksburg paper, the "Weekly Sun," of May 13th, 1861, which ridicules our enfeebled and unprepared condition, and says: "An official report made to Governor Yates, of Illinois, by one Captain Grant, says that after examining all the State armories he finds the muskets amount to just nine hundred and four, and of them only sixty in serviceable condition." Now the name of that man, who was looking up the rusty muskets in Illinois, is glory-crowned with shining victories, and will fill thousands of history's brightest pages to the end of time. I know well the secret of his power, for afterwards, when I saw him at head quarters, upon the march, and on the battle field, in his plain, thread-bare uniform, modest in his deportment, careful of the wants of the humblest soldier, personally inspecting all the dispositions and divisions of his army, calm and courageous amidst the most destructive fire of the enemy, it was evident that he had the confidence of every man, from the highest officer down to the humblest drummer boy in his whole command. His Generalship rivals that of Alexander and Napoleon, and his armies eclipse those of Greece and Rome, in their proudest days of imperial grandeur. He is a gift of the Almighty Father to THE NATION, in its extremity, and he has won his way to the exalted position he occupies through his own great perseverance, skill and indomitable bravery, and it is inexcusably vain for any man to claim that he has made Grant, or that he has given Grant to the country, or that he can control his great genius and deeds for the private ends of selfish and corrupt political ambition.

WAR EXPENDITURES.

The inability of the government to clothe, arm, subsist, transport and pay the first quota of troops, devolved upon the State extensive expenditures.

The Legislature, specially convened in April, 1861, provided for supplying troops raised under the first calls, and passed laws authorising the issuing of bonds to defray war expenses, and the appointment of a Board of Army Officers, to audit accounts. This board were governed by the provisions of the State law in adjusting war claims, and, upon their recommendation, approved by the Governor, the Auditor issued warrants on the Treasurer to claimants. The difficulty of getting accounts of the State adjusted, and reimbursements from the United States, created the necessity of frequent journeys to Washington, by myself and agents, as it was found impossible, in the immense pressure upon the departments, to accomplish much without persistent personal application. It was at length found necessary to adopt the plan of other States, and appoint a State agent there. Hon. Thos. H. Campbell, formerly State

Auditor, was appointed, and gave constant attention to the settlement of the State accounts, up to the time of his death. Afterwards, Hon. James C. Conkling was employed to go to Washington and press the settlement of our accounts, and succeeded in procuring payment of sufficient sums to relieve the Treasurer from the pressure of claimants holding warrants on the war fund. But owing to the immense pressure of business upon the Treasury Department, and difficulties experienced in making satisfactory explanations of accounts suspended and disallowed, he found it impossible, at the time of his last visit, to secure a final adjustment of our claims.

In March, 1864, I sent Col. John S. Loomis, who had been connected with the State Department from the commencement of the war—first as Assistant Adjutant General, and recently, as my principal Aid-de-Camp—to Washington, with instructions to urge final adjustment of all our accounts. His extensive acquaintance with the origin and history of our military organization and contracting and settlement of war claims, enabled him to make full explanation of our vouchers, and prosecute appeals from what was considered erroneous decisions of adjusting officers of the Treasury, in disallowing and suspending a part of our claims. He was accompanied by Gen. John Wood, Quartermaster General of the State, whose services were required to aid settlement of the class of claims originating in his department. From the report of Col. Loomis, and copies of his appeals on suspended and disallowed accounts, herewith transmitted, it will be seen that the claims of the State against the government, filed in the Treasury Department, for war expenses, amounted to three millions eight hundred and twelve thousand five hundred and twenty-five dollars and fifty-four cents ($3,812,525 54); of which amount there has been allowed, on various settlements with the Third Auditor, three millions seven hundred and twenty-six thousand seven hundred and ninety-two dollars and eighty-seven cents ($3,726,792 87) ; leaving a difference between the claims and allowances, in that department, of eighty-five thousand seven hundred and thirty-two dollars and sixty-seven cents ($85,732 67) suspended and disallowed, because, in the opinion of the said Auditor the law did not sufficiently provide for them. Of the amount allowed by the Third Auditor, and passed to the Second Comptroller of the Treasury, it will also be seen, that the Comptroller suspended nearly all of our State claims upon ground of insufficiency of vouchers, but which decision, upon the appeal of Col. Loomis, the Secretary of the Treasury reversed, and ordered a settlement of the accounts. An appeal was also taken upon the suspension and disallowment of accounts in the Third Auditor's office ($85,732 67), which is set forth in the report.

I am recently advised, by letter from the Treasury Department, that upon last settlement there was found to be due the State four hundred and sixty-eight thousand two hundred and sixty-five dollars and ninety-eight cents, ($468,265 98,) and that the amount of suspensions and disallowances has been reduced to twenty-seven thousand three hundred and ninety dollars and seventy-four cents, ($ 27,390 74.)

Thirty thousand dollars have recently been paid by the government on the balance found due on our accounts; which sum is sufficient to pay off all warrants drawn upon the State Treasury against the war fund.

There being no provision made by the Legislature for paying contingent expenses of the State government or for expenses of prosecuting claims against the government, the expenses incurred since the death of Mr. Campbell have been advanced by these agents, who should be reimbursed by the State.

In this connection, I desire to call your attention specially to the report of Colonel Loomis. It gives a complete history of a necessity for all the expenses incurred by the State for the General Government, and, in my opinion, clearly establishes the right of the State to reimbursement of every dollar we have advanced, and which yet remain suspended. Colonel Loomis' labors in the adjustment of our war accounts have been invaluable, and it is recommended that a sufficient appropriation be made for his services and expenses.

REPORT OF THE ADJUTANT GENERAL.

I regret that on account of the severe illness of Adjutant General A. C. Fuller, in November and December last, he has been unable to submit his regular biennial report. I transmit herewith a communication from him, exhibiting the expenses of his department during the past two years, the inadequate appropriations made by the Legislature to meet such expenses, and the amount required to pay the balance due various persons therein mentioned, and I recommend that an appropriation be made at an early day to pay it.

I have also lately inspected the Adjutant General's office, and deem it proper to say, that it is as complete in all its arrangements and in the perfection of its system and method as any similar office in the United States. General Fuller has been a most able, faithful and energetic officer, and is entitled to the gratitude of the State.

THE STATE SANITARY COMMISSION.

During the first year of the war our soldiers in the field received their supplies of sanitary stores principally through "Soldiers' Aid Societies," which were established in different parts of the State, and operated by the loyal women of Illinois, and the very pratical and patriotic munificence of citizens of Chicago, who established the "Sanitary Commission of Chicago." The operations of all these societies were conducted on the most liberal scale, and were in the highest degree useful. Almost every village and neighborhood in the State were engaged in the noble work. Humane and large hearted men contributed bountiful supplies of money and material, and loyal and patriotic women plied the needle and prepared articles of food and stores of every description, indispensable to the soldier; and the agents of these noble men and women covered the field with ambulances and filled the hospitals with appliances for the sick and wounded. These Soldiers' Aid Societies were the nucleus for all the great sanitary fairs which have so bountifully replenished the treasuries of the United States and Christian Commissions.

The government, in the early part of the war, depended upon the States for supplies for the regiments of each State entering the United States service, and from the embarrassed position attendant upon the organization of so large an army, it was impossible to provide so many at the right time and place with sanitary supplies. Appeals came to me, as Governor of the State, from agents already in the field, and from surgeons and commanding officers, urging the forwarding of sanitary stores, and I deemed it my duty to render the aid of the State to the extent of my power, by sending relief to the brave men who had with such enthusiasm and patriotic devotion to country, to peril health, life and property for the preservation of the Union.

On the 20th of August, 1862, I established a State Sanitary Bureau, and assigned charge of the department to Colonel John Williams, Commissary General of the State, to whom all communications and supplies were to be sent and distributed. I then addressed a circular to the people of the State of Illinois, soliciting contributions of money and supplies, and requesting them to forward them to this commission. As proof of the liberal response of the people, both in money and supplies, I take pleasure in referring you to the comprehensive report of Colonel Williams, set forth in "Report of Transactions of the Illinois State Sanitary Bureau," and transmitted herewith, and I take special pleasure in referring to the patient labors of Colonel Williams, who, during these long years of war, has afforded me invaluable advice and assistance in discharging our mutual obligations to the people and the army. Upon his advice and the enlarged and extensive field of usefulness prepared for us by the liberality of the people, in subscriptions, I changed the organization of the Sanitary Bureau on the 12th day of September, 1863, by establishing the "Illinois State Sanitary Commission," with Colonel John Williams, Hon. William Butler, John P. Reynolds, Esq., Robert Irwin, Esq., and Eliphalet B. Hawley, Esq., constituted as a Board of Directors, to supervise and control the operations of the Commission, and referred to this board the annual report of the "Sanitary Bureau," embracing a complete statement of receipts and disbursements of stores and moneys contributed by citizens of the State for sanitary purposes. The "Sanitary Bureau," to this time, had received, in addition to a large amount of sanitary stores, twenty-eight thousand dollars, ($28,000,) and expended twenty thousand dollars, ($20,000,) leaving a balance of eight thousand dollars ($8,000) to be transferred to the treasury of the "Illinois State Sanitary Commission." A statement of the receipts and disbursements of this commission, from its organization to the 31st day of December, 1863, will be found in the joint report of the "State Sanitary Bureau" and "Illinois State Sanitary Commission," before referred to, and transactions since that time will soon be communicated to your honorable body.

The time and services of all the directors of the "State Commission" have been given gratuitously, and they have been most faithful and worthy custodians of the people's bounty to our brave boys in the field.

I may be pardoned for doing merited justice to the aid societies of Quincy, Jacksonville, Springfield, Alton, Bloomington, Decatur, Peoria, Galesburg, and other cities and towns throughout the State, and especially to our metropolitan city of Chicago, which through her Board of Trade, her various sanitary associations, Soldiers' Aid Societies, and individual efforts of many of her citizens have rendered most munificent aid, and, in this respect, has fully come up to that high standard, which in so many other matters of patriotic and public spirited enterprise, has given her justly a proud rank among the first cities of the Union.

REPORTS OF SANITARY AGENTS.

I refer the General Assembly to the very interesting reports of our sanitary agents, and more especially to the reports of Colonel T. P. Robb, who has been agent for the State from the commencement of the war, and whose labors have been most severe, arduous and efficient. I recommend that a large number of his reports be printed and circulated for information of the people. The reports of Dr. O. M. Long, State Agent at New Orleans, Edward I. Eno, at Nashville, and Mr. Dunseth, at Louisville, and some others which I submit, contain valuable information. I also recommend that the Legislature make proper appropriations for their services and expenditures.

STATE ARSENAL.

During the four years past, vast quantities of ammunition have been fabricated at the arsenal, for field guns and small arms for the General Government. Arms have been repaired, cleaned and stored, and nearly all the arms used by the various arms of the service in the field from this State, have been received, stored and issued through the Engineer-in-Chief of the State. The State arsenal, for the most part, has been used as an ordnance depot for the General Government. Frequently the arsenal has had stored within it more than a million dollars worth of valuable property. Much and constant labor has been given, in arming and equipping the various regiments of the State. All the regiments for the three months' service were armed and equipped from its stores; also, all the arms of the various veteran regiments have been received and stored, and, at the expiration of furloughs, re-issued by the officer in charge of the department. The arsenal, located in the midst of the city, in which is stored a large quantity of materials liable to explode at any moment, has given rise to much dissatisfaction on the part of the citizens living in the immediate vicinity. Quite recently, two fires occurred in the frame buildings adjacent, and it was saved from destruction only by prompt efforts and the removal of a stable adjoining. In view of the complaints, which seem to be well grounded, I would respectfully suggest that the General Assembly, in the exercise of sound discretion, take such steps for its removal, or the building of a larger and more suitable ordnance depot, beyond the limits of the city.

I would also recommend that a sufficient appropriation be made, to reimburse the party, the destruction of whose property was necessary to save the arsenal.

I cannot speak in too high terms of Col. W. D. Crowell, the officer in charge of the arsenal. He has shown the utmost faithfulness and ability in the discharge of his duties.

THE MILITIA.

I will not discuss the importance of a military organization of the State further than to refer you to my former messages on this subject, and to add my firm conviction that it is the duty of this General Assembly to pass a law providing for putting the State upon a complete military footing. There have been times, during my administration, when I felt the want of such a law. The raids into Pennsylvania by Lee, and into Indiana and Ohio, when those States had no military organization to meet them, show that our statesmen have not paid much attention to the safe maxim, "in peace prepare for war." The threatened raids upon the Ohio at Paducah and Shawneetown, were sufficient to create general alarm. If Forrest had been successful at Paducah, or Price had been successful in Missouri, they would have looked to the rich fields of Illinois for conquest and plunder. The first duty of every citizen is to the State, and, therefore, let the General Assembly enact such laws as will, in case of emergency, upon the shortest notice, secure the services of every able-bodied citizen to the State. At my request, one of our best and ablest officers, Colonel John M. Loomis, late of the 26th Illinois infantry, has commenced the preparation of a bill, which he will, if desired, submit to the committee on military affairs, for their consideration.

RECORD OF ILLINOIS SOLDIERS.

I would recommend to the Legislature that a work be prepared and published, giving the name, age, residence, occupation, nativity, date of enlistment and muster of every Illinois soldier engaged in government service during this war. Also, a historical memoranda, embracing the casualties to officers and men, and the marches, skirmishes and battles in which each company and regiment have participated, and the different brigade, division, army corps and departments to which they have been attached during their term of service. This record could be compiled from rolls and files of the Adjutant General's office, and reports from the field, which could, with proper attention, be procured. To secure an accurate history of men and organizations, the work should be immediately commenced, and finished before regiments now in service are disbanded on expiration of term of enlistment. The work would be of priceless value to our State for all time, and would remain the most glorious history of the part we have taken in the war for defense of the Union, that could possibly be written. I sincerely hope the Legislature will seriously consider and carry out this recommendation.

RECOMMENDATIONS FOR TAX FOR DESTITUTE FAMILIES OF SOLDIERS, SCHOOLS FOR SOLDIERS' ORPHANS, AND A STATE SANITARY BUREAU.

I solicit the earnest consideration of the General Assembly to several important propositions. First—that a tax be levied of not less than two mills to the dollar during the continuance of the war, for the relief of the destitute families of our deceased and disabled soldiers. In some states, large provision has been made by the Legislature for this object, while in ours none has been made. The cases of actual suffering which have come to my notice have been very numerous. Ohio levies a tax of two mills on the dollar for this purpose. Illinois is not a parsimonious people, and while no state has beat her in the valor of her troops, I trust none shall in the generosity of her people. Second—that a State Sanitary

—5

Bureau be established, and ample appropriation be made for sending efficient agents to all the principal points where our troops are operating to distribute supplies, or to see that our troops receive their full share of the supplies from this State which are required to be distributed through the United States Sanitary Commission; also to visit our sick and wounded, and minister to their wants on the battle-field, to aid them in procuring furloughs, discharges, pay, etc. Indeed, I think that an agent might be usefully employed in accompanying each regiment of Illinois Volunteers, for the purpose of taking care of the sick, burying the dead, marking the spot of burial and corresponding with the friends and government at home, and making an annual report to the Adjutant General's office of the condition, wants, sufferings and achievements of the regiment. Under the supervision of this Bureau might be established a claim agency, through which all claims, pensions and bounties might be collected, free of cost to the claimant.

Second—each county court should be vested with authority to erect a monument to the officers and soldiers from that county who had died from wounds received in battle.

Third—that a stipulated sum be appropriated by a well digested enactment of this General Assembly, with all the proper details, guards and restrictions, setting apart a fund to erect buildings and endow an institution as a home for the maintenance and education of the orphan children of our deceased or disabled soldiers, or that the said fund be properly distributed for their support, and their education in the district schools of the State.

At Chicago, Quincy, Mattoon, and other places in the State, patriotic and benevolent individuals have already made large subscriptions towards the erection of homes for the orphan children of our soldiers, which entitles them to the gratitude of the country, and while very much has been, and doubtless will be done by patriotic and benevolent men and women in this direction, I appeal to the General Assembly not to suffer the performance of this great duty to depend upon the uncertain contingency of private benevolence.

If this government, with its million blessings, is to be secured to us, and transmitted to future generations, it will be done by our soldiers. If the army saves the republic, should there not be something like adequate remuneration to the men who have sacrificed so much for the country? and should not we who have remained at home, having a million bayonets between us and danger, enjoying all the blessings of peace, and many actually reaping benefits besides from the war, in all kinds of business revived, provide for the comfort of their families? These brave boys comprise the flower of the commonwealth—are as intelligent and worthy as we. Many of them have left wives and children dependent upon them for support, and, with the present scanty pay, they find it impossible to keep them from penury, and I know hundreds of instances of actual suffering. It would be a burning shame if the exercise of noble devotion of our citizens, who are willing to give up their homes, their wives and children, should be the cause of suffering to those dearer to them than life. Let the provision be ample enough for every child in Illinois who can say, "my father fell at Belmont, or at Donelson, or Shiloh, or Corinth, or Vicksburg, Stone River, Chattanooga, Mission Ridge, Mobile, the capture of Richmond, the siege and destruction of Charleston, or the last grand triumphant struggle between freedom and slavery." It is no charity that I ask you to bestow upon them—it is your *duty* to take notice of every household saddened by the loss of a father or son in this war, and no man can enjoy the blessings of an approving conscience in this life, or the hope of salvation hereafter, who dares to neglect them. If the country will not take care of and provide for them, we are unworthy the sacrifices of our patriot sires of the revolution, and the shining record of manly courage and lofty patriotism of the Union armies of this day. No State is worthy of its sovereignty, and no government the respect of its people, who will not protect and nurture the children of its soldiers. No marble shaft marks the spot where sleep in the valley of the Cumberland or Tennessee, or on the banks of the father of waters, the remains of the brave Illinois volunteer, but we will most honor the dead by taking care of the living; and I speak in the name of the loyal millions of Illinois when I say that in all the ranks of the destitute children of our fallen and disabled soldiers, not one shall be left to beg or grow up in ignorance for want of an education. Illinois! the first upon the roll of honor among all the States, shall she not be among the first to emblazon her proud historic record by setting apart a liberal and unfailing endowment for the support and education of the indigent orphans of the soldiers of the State?

52

SOLDIERS' NATIONAL CEMETERY AT GETTYSBURG.

In August, 1863, shortly after the battle of Gettysburg, Pennsylvania, it was proposed by the Governor of Pennsylvania, that a National Cemetery should be establised at Gettysburg, for the burial of all the Union soldiers killed in said battle. This proposition was made to the Governors of all those States whose soldiers had participated in the battle, to wit: the States of Maine, New Hampshire, Vermont, Massachusetts, Rhode Island, Connecticut, New York, New Jersey, Pennsylvania, Delaware, Maryland, Ohio, Indiana, Wisconsin, Michigan, Minnesota and Illinois; and in it was embodied a plan for the establishment of the cemetery, which provides for the purchase of the ground, transfer of the bodies, and the establishment and maintenance of the cemetery, and also for the erection of a suitable monument, and the expenses for the establishment and maintenance of the cemetery, etc., to be apportioned among the States having soldiers buried there, each State to be assessed according to its population, as indicated by its representation in Congress. Without express authority, I deemed it my duty to join the Executives of other States named, in the acceptance of the plan, and thus securing to the noble sons of Illinois who had lost their lives in that sanguinary struggle a suitable resting place. The grounds were accordingly purchased and laid out by the State of Pennsylvania, and in November, 1863, I appointed Messrs. Clark E. Carr, of Galesburg, and Wm. L. Church, of Chicago, commissioners, to represent the State of Illinois at the inauguration ceremonies, which took place on the 19th of November, 1863. I would call your attention to all the correspondence on this subject herewith submitted, and the interesting report of the commissioners, which will be submitted to you.

I doubt not that my action in thus accepting, in behalf of the people of the State, a proposition securing to their brave dead a resting place and a monument worthy of their gallant deeds, will be approved, and that an appropriation will be made by the General Assembly of the proportionate share of Illinois, to be paid to the treasurer of the National Cemetery Association, in such installments as may be called for by the officers of the association; and also that an appropriation be made to pay the expenses of the commissioners, as set forth in their report.

In my inaugural and messages I presented at length my views upon the causes and remedies for the political troubles in which our country is involved. I shall now only refer to the present military situation, and to the hopeful prospects from the emphatic endorsement of the measures of the administration at the late election. Of the former, it is sufficient to say that, without feeling the first symptoms of exhaustion in the free loyal states, our arms are everywhere victorious, upon the land and upon the sea. We have lost no important ground; we have reclaimed the larger part of the territory and national property which had been taken from us. Grant has driven the enemy, step by step, from its siege of Washington to the gates of Richmond; Sheridan has swept clean the valley of the Shenandoah, driving Early backward, no more to lay waste our borders; Farragut remains undisputed conqueror of the seas; Sherman dashes, with Napoleonic tramp, and roams unrestrained, from city to city, through the very heart of the confederacy, unfurls our flag defiantly in the face of Charleston—soon to wave in re-established glory upon the very hights from which traitor hands struck it. And the very latest, perhaps the cleanest and most glorious victory of the war, displaying the most indomitable valor and brilliant achievements of our troops, is that of General Thomas and his brave army. The bonds of the confederacy are worthless in their own and every foreign market, all hope of foreign intervention or northern revolution, has failed them, and to-day our nation stands under brighter skies than have smiled upon us since the inauguration of the President on the 4th day of March, 1861, and before us the cheering prospect of speedy and final victory.

The verdict of the American people, at the late election, solved finally and forever all the questions of doubt as to the policy which is hereafter to be pursued. The history of the world presents no such grand results achieved in the interests of human liberty as that presented on the 8th day of November last, when the people, in the face of heavy taxation and enormous debt, in the face of immense sacrifice of life and treasure, when, amidst the trials, stress and storms of civil war, and the most intense political excitement, they went in almost breathless quiet to the polls, and recorded their solemn verdict upon all the controverted questions which before have divided and agitated the country.

The result of that election has defeated all the hopes and expectations of the rebel leaders. Vice President Stephens, by far the greatest of all the insurgent leaders, confidently looked to divided counsels in the north as almost the last and only hope of success. But the verdict of the American people has declared, in language which does not admit of misconstruction, an invincible determination to prosecute the war to the bitter end of their final subjugation and annihilation, if they wickedly persist in their purposes and efforts to overthrow the government.

Every patriot contemplates with gratitude to God the safe passage of the nation through the ordeal of the Presidential election. We were in the midst of a terrible war—a fierce party contest was raging in all the loyal states, with personal hatreds and private ambition, and every element calculated to fan into frenzy the popular passions—there were ominous threatenings of civil war in the free states—the enemies of our government, in Europe as well as in the disloyal states, expected and predicted fatal divisions, and loyal men everywhere held their breath, in anxious fear of anarchy and disruption. But universal quiet everywhere prevailed, and peace, like the breath of spring, settled upon all the territory of the loyal states; and be it recorded as one of the sublimest spectacles in history, that the defeated party cheerfully acquiesced in the will of the majority. It is a pleasure now to record that, whether the minority was right or wrong before the election, they are all right now, and all bow in reverence and submission to the decisions of the ballot box—and whether they do believe the measures of the administration were the best or not, they yield a cheerful acquiescence, and evince every determination to stand by the authorities, and prosecute the war with the utmost vigor, because such is the verdict of the people.

I am far from disposed to consider the triumph at the late election in the light of a mere party triumph. It was a national victory. The enemies of the government need not lay the flattering unction to their souls that, because there was not perfect unanimity, there was any great division upon the leading question of the war, whether the Union shall be preserved. It would be absurd, and maliciously false, as well as detracting from the strength of the nation, to denominate as rebels all who have differed with the measures and policy of the government. It is but justice to say of our fellow citizens in Illinois, who constitute the minority, that however they differed from us as to the men and measures of the administration, yet by far the larger part of them had convictions as strong and deep as our own in favor of the preservation of our glorious Union, and that to-day the sentiment of the free loyal states approximates closely to a unit in favor of all the leading principles of our republican institutions. This important fact is evidence of our national strength, and a warning to traitors and tyrants that though our people do not vote alike, yet they feel, think and will act alike upon the main question of preserving unbroken our nationality.

It teaches to foreign nations that there is an intense and undivided sentiment in favor of the preservation of the Union at every hazard of human life and national treasure, and that while the United States desires and prays for peace with all the world, she is not so divided as to brook any interference from any foreign government, potentate or power, in the adjustment of the question whether she shall require and enforce obedience to her constitution and laws. And protesting that peace is our desire and not war, I speak in behalf of the two millions of Illinois, when I say that they stand ready to repel with the strong arm of military power, interference from any foreign country, or any of its dependencies; and that we will meet them on the land or on the sea, whenever they seek to try the issue. We mind our own business, let foreign nations mind theirs. We ask no favors, nothing but the neutrality which every nation interested to maintain its national authority must have, and that we will have or we will have war. Such language is not diplomatic, but it is the feeling of every true hearted American, who has reluctantly been forced to believe that through jealousy of our growing power and our free and liberal institutions, the two great nations of Europe have not only sympathized with but contributed material aid to the rebels in their attempt to overthrow our government. For such offences the United States has too long been paid with diplomatic apologies. The United States could well overlook the unauthorized acts of reckless British sailors and bravadoes; but British statesmen, men of rank and power, the large portion of the British nobility and the government press have from the beginning of the war exhibited to our cause bitter hostility and rejoiced in the reverses to our arms. They have friend-ly connivance to vessels which ran our blockades, and to pirates who preyed upon our commerce; have suffered piratical ships to be built in her ports, and to be manned with sailors from her navy, and our brave boys fighting for the Union have been shot by Eng-lish cannon and English muskets placed in the hands of the rebels by British gold. Rebel ambassadors and conspirators have been feted and lionized at British courts, while our ministers have been treated with the cold formalities of diplomatic intercourse. In a neighboring British province traitors from the south and the north, and foreign emissaries, have holden their counsel of treason and conspiracy against our government, while southern traitors have sought the protection of English soil from which to send their raid-ers to burn our vessels on the lakes and rob and murder our citi-zens.

Now our only reliance for a continuation of peace with England is thorough and ample preparation for war. We cannot calculate upon her justice when her sympathies and prejudices are so marked against us. Our immunity from war with England is in our strength. Our policy and our safety is to let it be made apparent to England and all foreign nations that we ask no favors, and that we can make war more destructive to them than they can to us. While we ap-peal to their justice, we will let them understand that we expect it more from the strength of our naval marine and the calibre of our guns, than from any fair foreign appreciation of our cause. In this connexion I recommend the General Assembly to express in strong terms their approval of the action of the President, that af-ter the expiration of the six months conditionally stipulated in the arrangement with Great Britian, the United States will proceed to increase her naval armament upon the lakes. The State of Illinois, as well as every State bordering upon the lakes, is deeply inter-ested in this question. Our cities and harbors are exposed to raids and incursions without vessels of war to protect them. Indeed, the power to control the northern lakes is now in the hands of the British government, because by her canals she could in a few weeks place a fleet of gunboats upon them by which she could an-nihilate our commerce and place all of our lake cities, without a single exception, at the mercy of the invader. And here also is the war argument in favor of our own ship canal, by which we could transfer our fleets of gunboats, transports and munitions of war from our seaboard to the lakes, if required by the emergency of war with a foreign nation.

But again, the verdict of the people at the late election is the death of the traitorous theory of secession. It reasserts the doctrine of our fathers, as maintained in the late Baltimore platform, that the Union is not a mere compact or league from which any State may recede at its mere caprice or pleasure : and we send down to our children our solemn verdict that the national government is the sovereign power of the land—that the constitution of the United States and the laws made in pursuance thereof shall be the supreme law of the land. There is no political heresy so dangerous to the existence of our government as the doctrine of the right of secession which southern politicians have sugar coated with the plausible sobriquet of State Sovereignty. The theory is full of danger—of inevitable national disintegration and final overthrow. Were I to presume to leave a lesson to my children most serviceable to my country, it would be to guard against the insidious doctrine of State sovereignty in the meaning which nearly all southern politicians and many northern politicians have given to it. To understand the immense danger, look at the action of Governor Seymour, who during the war has thrown the power of the Empire State of the Union against the constituted authorities of the government, and consequently against a vigorous prosecution of the war, under an hypocritical pretense that his action was dictated by a controlling desire to preserve the rights of the States from federal usurpation.

The motto of the State of Illinois is " State Sovereignty and National Union," which, properly understood, is, in my estimation, the best and most beautiful motto which adorns the armorial bearings of any State in the Union. I am for unlimited state sovereignty in the true sense : in the sense that the State is to control and direct all its municipal and local legislation ; and I would be among the first to resist all attempts upon the part of the Federal Government to interpose tyrannical usurpation of power in controlling the legislation of the States. The States are sovereign, in every sense in which it is desirable they should have sovereignty : that is, the people know and understand their immediate wants, social, agricultural, commercial, mechanical, educational, municipal ; and the interference of Congress, except in aid of these, with the consent of the people of the States, would be a flagrant abuse of power, which every patriot son of Illinois would resist with all his energies, and *all* his life. But how immensely absurd is the idea that the people of the States should unite together, and form a written constitution, and constitute a national government, with representation from the people from every State, and confer upon that government all the powers of peace and war, and every power, in fact, which affected the safety and prosperity of all the States, and all the people, as one nationality, and constitute a Congress to make the laws necessary for the government of the whole—an executive, chosen from all the people, to execute the laws, and a judiciary composed of men, residents of the different states, and declare the constitution and laws the supreme authority in the land, to decide the questions at variance between the government and the States, and between the several States themselves, and yet admit that any State may, at its mere pleasure, peaceably withdraw from the Union. Such was the doctrine of the old confederacy. The States first formed a confederacy in the nature of a mere league; but, being found ineffectual, a constitution was formed by the people of the States for a more perfect union, for the express purpose of doing away with the principle of unlimited State sovereignty.

I hail it as the most important result of our glorious war that the doctrine of the fathers has been re-asserted, and that, while we are opposed to a monarchy or to a consolidated government, which would ignore the existence of state sovereignty, yet we recognize as essential to union and national perpetuity, the centralization somewhere of a power which shall be the arbiter in the case of disagreement between the States. Otherwise, indeed, our government is a rope of sand. If any one will carefully study the form of our government, he will see the necessity of the checks and balances which our fathers threw around it; for there are two powers in constant and increasing conflict, and if a fair equilibrium is not maintained, the government is lost. In the solar system, the sun holds the planets in their orbits, and, but for its power, each planet would fly off darkling through the realms of space; but if its power were uncontrolled, and above all the laws of forces and equilibrium, it would, by the force of natural gravity, draw every planet headlong into the central orb, which would be consolidation, and resemble the despotism and powers of Europe. But, on the other hand, if the sun were to lose its supremacy altogether, and the planets should become the supreme forces, they would fly off lawless through the void, producing wild anarchy in the solar system, which nothing but the Almighty Power, who created them and all things, could subdue. Our only safety is in the hope that these forces, in our State and national governments, will balance each other; that, in strict obedience to constitutional law, the States will perform their duties to their own citizens, to each other, and to the whole nation; and that the national government will commit no usurpation of state privileges. The careful observer of our government will perceive that the tendency is not to consolidation, but to anarchy and dissolution. The rapidity in growth and population of the States, makes them feel their consequence and strength more, and their dependence less sensibly on the Federal Government; like the high-spirited youth who feels less dependent, from day to day, as he approximates the age of his majority.

Indeed, we may say that our government is fearfully and wonderfully made, and the great machine of state must move, self-poised, magnificently onward between the dead calm of consolidation and the convulsions of anarchy and disunion.

The late election has settled all disputed questions. It is settled that traitors may be arrested and hung; it is settled that the first duty of every citizen is to his country, and that he may be drafted into the military service; it is settled that men, irrespective of color, may be employed in the military service of the country.

But, again, this election has settled the great question of slavery. It has indorsed the proclamation of the President, and all the measures of his administration tending to the emancipation of the slave. Whatever may have been the sentiment of the American people heretofore on the subject of slavery, it cannot be denied that they have fully resolved that it must cease to exist in every State and Territory of the Union.

I have ever believed that the slavery question was the source of all our national troubles; that it was at war with the genius of our institutions, and that we can never have permanent peace and a harmonious Union without its thorough eradication; and while statesmen of the highest standing, and many good men everywhere, have feared lest radical measures might endanger the unity of the friends of the government, and that some end short of radical and universal emancipation was the best policy of the government, and necessary to the preservation of the Union, yet I have ever believed, and now believe, that it is in the councils of a higher power than man that this rebellion will know no end except upon the basis of unconditional and universal emancipation. In fact, I may go further and say that I scarce desire to see this war terminated with this disturbing element left to divide our councils, to embroil citizen against citizen and State against State, to result in another bloody war and perhaps in final disunion. I do not desire to see the war terminated until it shall be a recognized fact—recognized not only by our own government, but by the Confederate States, including both government and people, and be made patent to all the civilized nations of the world, that not under the constitution of the United States—not under any constitution or law of any seceded State—not under any decision of any legal tribunal, State or National—and not even in any conventional, moral, social or individual sense, shall the relation of slave and master, in the form of absolute submission on the one hand and uncontrolled ownership on the other hand, be recognized upon any portion of North American soil. Already reeling and tottering beneath the blows it has already received, it is our duty to give this accursed wrong and cause of all our sufferings a final blow, and send it to a grave from which it will have no resurrection. When the shout of victory comes to us from Grant, or Sherman's armies, we rejoice, because we consider each victory brings us nearer peace and the restored authority of the government. We rejoice when we hear that Atlanta, Mobile or Savannah is ours, but I shall consider peace nearer when, either through the legislation of Congress or from the act of our armies, or of the rebels themselves, slavery is destroyed. It is significant to me of victory when I see the recent movement of the south towards organizing the negroes into regiments, putting arms into their hands, and giving them their freedom. It is a strange phenomenon in history: the leaders of an insurrection calling upon the cause of that insurrection to save it. Driven to madness and despair, they themselves commence putting down their "divine institution" for which they commenced the war. Providence is shaping their destiny so that with their own hands they shall bring to destruction the very thing that they meant to maintain, and which they designed to make the permanent corner-stone of their new confederacy. Of what use will a new government be to the rebels when their slaves are free, and when they can have no use for it?

I am for freeing the negro by every constitutional means; and I believe, as I ever did, that had the seceded States behaved themselves—had they been true and loyal to the Government—they had from all the people of all the loyal States an unfailing guarantee of non-intervention in their domestic institutions. Indeed, very few if any prominent statesmen believed that Congress had any power whatever to interfere with the institution of slavery. But what government may lawfully do, in time of peace, against its own citizens who are loyal to the government, and what it may lawfully do towards those citizens in time of war, when they themselves have thrown off their allegiance to the government, and become open and diabolical enemies of that government, is quite another thing. To illustrate: the humblest American citizen has rights which the whole American government and all the powers of darkness cannot deprive him of while he is a good, loyal citizen and obeys the laws of his country. To him, personal liberty and protection is a sacred right, which the lordliest in the land dare not infringe with impunity; but if he violates the law—if he commits theft or murder—if he becomes an outlaw—then he may be deprived of his personal liberty. So, although it was in the bond that slavery should not be interfered with in the States, yet when those States and the people break the bond—trample the very constitution and laws, which were the shield of their protection, under their feet—deny their allegiance to that constitution, take up arms to overthrow the government, and become the public enemies of the country—then the government may take that man's life, or his property of any and every kind, if necessary, to compel his submission and save the government. And, therefore, I have no doubt of the power of Congress, in such a case, to pass a broad, manly act of emancipation, breaking the chains of every slave in every seceded State; and my doctrine is the immediate, total abolition of slavery in every seceded State.

Of course, Congress would have no power to abolish slavery in the loyal and adhering States, without their consent, and hence the necessity of an amendment to the constitution, by which slavery shall be abolished in every State, loyal as well as disloyal, under the forms and in the manner prescribed by the Constitution—and thus free the whole land forever from the everlasting curse of human bondage. It will be one of the earliest duties, I trust, of your honorable bodies, to urge upon Congress immediate action upon the proposed amendment of the constitution abolishing slavery throughout the United States. During the last session of Congress it passed, by a majority of two-thirds in the Senate, both the Senators from Maryland, both the Senators from West Virginia, and both the Senators from Missouri, and a large majority of the Senators representing slave States voting for it. In the House it failed for want of a two-thirds vote, and lacked only eleven votes of passing, so that, although the same Congress is to sit again, this winter, yet so emphatic has been the verdict of the people in its favor, as to induce the belief that there will be enough members, who opposed it before, to conform to the national will and carry it through the present Congress; but if they do not, then the next Congress, already elected upon that issue, will carry the measure triumphantly through. Then it will be part of the organic law of the republic, wiping out the last blot upon the fair charter of our freedom—universal freedom for all—everywhere under the folds of our starry banner.

It is perhaps difficult to tell in how many new and different phases the question may during the next two years assume—how many plans for gradual or half-way emancipation—how many compromises may be devised by politicians, but I confidently trust that the voice of Illinois shall be ever living and potential, through her honored representatives in the General Assembly, for the most direct and shortest route to radical and universal emancipation.

Another lesson taught by the late election was, that the war shall be vigorously prosecuted until every armed rebel shall lay down his arms and submit to the rightful authority of the government, and until our national flag shall wave in triumph over all our broad territory in all its geographical bounds, one and unbroken, from gulf to gulf, and from ocean to ocean. The triumph of the war policy at the polls is the triumph of the war itself. It never has been a question in the mind of any sound statesman or general, whether we had the power to conquer the rebels into obedience to the government; the only question was whether we would do it—and we have now decided the question of the result of the war by the emphatic announcement of the people that they intend to fight the war through—yes! fight it through, and settle all questions in dispute for all time to come. No one can fail to admire the wisdom and humanity of the President in his late message, wherein he says, in substance, that while he declines to hold out terms of negotiation to the insurgent leaders, yet he holds out the olive branch of peace to the masses who follow their leaders, and tell them that "they can at any moment have peace by laying down their arms and submitting to the national authority under the constitution." He says, "the door has been and is still open to all, but the time may come, probably, when public duty shall demand that it be closed, and in lieu, more vigorous measures than heretofore shall be adopted."

Now is a time, if ever, the nation can afford to be magnanimous, in view of our great strength and the unanimity of our people, as expressed at the recent election—in view of the fact that the enemy is everywhere close pressed by our conquering legions— we can now, not taking counsel from our fears, but from our magnanimity and with the power of conscious strength, knowing that our final triumph is but a question of time, we can invite the deluded masses of the south to lay down their arms and come in again to share the protection and blessings of the government.

But in the mean time every effort should be made to push forward vigorously the car of war. Not for one moment should the executive stay his strong military arm in the suppression of the rebellion. The greatest calamity which could befall this country now; in fact the greatest danger to be apprehended is that, from the very consciousness of our strength and the speedy prospect of success, we may relax our efforts, and the war become a protracted, lazy, heavy, draggling war. Should such be the case, there is no telling what may be the final issue— what demoralization may seize our army—what divisions may spring up among the people—at what time foreign nations may consider it their duty to intervene, and finally what disgraceful compromise and dishonorable peace may be brought about, leaving all the blood and treasure of four years' terrible war to have been expended in vain. The only hope of the enemy is that we will fail to follow up the advantages already gained. If ever, *now* is the time to press forward with overwhelming demonstration of our national power and forces to the goal of speedy and final victory. *Onward* with the war. The people should demand it; every legislative assembly should press it upon Congress; Congress should press it upon the President, and the President upon the Generals in the army; the whole nation should wake up to the one great purpose, and resolve that there shall now be no lagging in the war. And while we hold out the words of kindness and the olive branch of peace to the south, let us resolve upon quick, sharp, decisive war, and besides paying liberal bounties to our soldiers at home, let us adopt the ancient mode of war, hold out to our boys in blue the sunny fields of the south, capture the territory, divide the lands among the soldiers, to be held by them and their heirs in fee simple forever. We have long held out this same olive branch by the proclamations of the President. The only answer has been insult and injury. The most savage cruelties have been heaped upon our prisoners in the hands of the enemy, and from Jeff. Davis has come the bold and defiant language that he will never consent to any peace—his voice is still for war until the United States shall acknowledge the independence of the Confederate States." Now I am here to-day to say in behalf of the loyal millions of Illinois, and I trust this General Assembly is prepared to say, and to throw in the face of Jeff. Davis and of his minions, and of all traitors who would destroy our Union, the determined response that in the booming thunders of Farragut's cannon, in the terrible onslaught of Sherman's legions, in the flaming sabres of Sheridan's cavalry, and in the red battle glare of Grant's artillery, our voice is still for war—war to the knife—all the dread enginery of war—persistent, unrelenting, stupendous, exterminating war, till the last rebel shall lay down his arms and our flag float in triumph over the land.

Upon the subject which agitates the minds of many, whether the north and south, after such deadly strife, can ever resume friendly relations and live in harmonious fellowship in one Union and under the same government, is a question which has never given me any doubt. Slavery has been the only ground of bitterness and division. All other questions were political and commercial, which all were ready to submit to the common arbitrament of the ballot; but the question of slavery was social, domestic and organic, and perhaps like all the questions involving the rights of man and the principles of liberty, which have engendered bloody wars in all ages and all nations. There could have been no solution to this question, except the war which has grown out of it. But slavery once removed, there will be an homogeneousness of sentiment, having the effect to bind together the north and the south.

The tides of emigration are already thrown into new channels. Emigration from the south to the north and from the north to the south now crosses each other at all our commercial points on our rivers and along all our thoroughfares of trade.

The black wall of slavery, which, like a frightful specter, drove the emigrant from the sunny fields and rich savannahs of the south, is, or soon will be, broken down—the process of intermixture, intermarriage, reciprocal business and commercial relations, will assume the place of the unsocial isolations which have heretofore divided the sections. And though the war has been bitter and bloody, yet the history of most nations of Europe teaches that they have survived long and bloody civil wars, and yet afterwards lived in peace and harmony under the same government. Such is the history of France, after her revolution. The civil war of England, in the memorable days of Cromwell, was marked by scenes of violence, of confiscation of property, of devastation of estates and desolation of towns and cities, as intense and terrible as those which have marked the progress of our civil war. Upon the re-establishment of the government, the people became united, and every memory of the rancour of the war soon disappeared. And so, after the vindication of our national authority, each section awarding to the other the credit due to lofty and indomitable prowess, like friends who have fought it out and are better friends ever after, so will the north and the south bury the memory of their wrongs. Massachusetts and Illinois will again reunite with Virginia and Georgia over the grave of treason, and together with the new-born sisters of the confederacy, will live on in the bonds of a new brotherhood, and with fresh allegiance to the constitution, and an unfailing faith in the proved strength of our institutions and man's capacity for self government, strengthened and reassured by the baptism of blood through which the nation has passed, they will move on as one people, united forever.

Such is to be the end of events passing before us, and I trust that the people of the United States, and their posterity, while they offer up praises and thanksgiving to Almighty God for the deliverance he has brought to our people out of this red sea of blood—they will bless with a nation's gratitude, from age to age, the memories of the brave men who have perilled all for their country in

—6

its dark and trying hour. And when our own Illinois, upon some national holiday, shall meet all our returning soldiers, as they shall pass in serried ranks, with their old battle scarred banners and shivered cannons, and rusty bayonets and sabres—with rebel flags and rebel trophies of every kind—at this mighty triumphal procession, surpassing the proudest festivals of ancient Rome and Greece, in their palmiest days, then the loud plaudits of a grateful people will go up: All hail to the veterans who have given our flag to the God of storms, the battle and the breeze, and consecrated our country afresh to union, liberty and humanity.

Gentlemen of the General Assembly: In taking my leave of the high responsibilities of the executive of this great State, I can congratulate you and the people that the administration of its affairs will pass into the hands of a successor who is fully competent to the trust committed to his care—who has given the highest evidence of devotion to the country, by both distinguished civil and military service—and in whose great ability, sound judgment and unswerving integrity I have the most entire confidence.

I cannot fail here to refer in kindness and gratitude to Lieutenant Governor Hoffman, who has been my constant adviser and counselor, and who has acted as Governor in my absence, with great ability and efficiency; and to my associate State officers, Hon. Jesse K. Dubois, Hon. O. M. Hatch and Hon. William Butler, to whom I am deeply indebted for wise counsel and cordial co-operation in important matters of my administration. Also, to Quartermaster General Ex-Governor John Wood, and Commissary General John Williams, for most indefatigable and efficient service; and also to the aid-de-camps in my office, and in the office of the Adjutant General, and to the clerks in all the departments of the State government, for their faithful and useful labors.

I must be indulged in saying that, while, doubtless, many omissions have occurred, and many errors have been committed, yet my labors have been severe and arduous, and that perplexities of a most difficult and unusual character, growing out of the unsettled condition of the country, have met me on every hand—among which was lack of co-operation in a co-ordinate branch of the government, and the want of adequate appropriations required in the new emergencies to be met by the Executive. However, I shall never regret the anxieties, cares and responsibilities which have devolved upon me, if, in some degree, I have discharged the high trust committed to me to the satisfaction of the people of the State.

RICHARD YATES.

January 2, 1865.